PETITIONS AND JUDGMENTS CECIL COUNTY COURT

1717–1732

Abstracts
with
Selected Transcriptions

Compiled by

John F. Polk, Ph.D.

HERITAGE BOOKS
2021

HERITAGE BOOKS

AN IMPRINT OF HERITAGE BOOKS, INC.

Books, CDs, and more—Worldwide

For our listing of thousands of titles see our website
at
www.HeritageBooks.com

.

Published 2021 by
HERITAGE BOOKS, INC.
Publishing Division
5810 Ruatan Street
Berwyn Heights, Md. 20740

Heritage Books by the author:

*Beyond Damned Quarter: The Polk/Pollock Family of
the Chesapeake Eastern Shore in the Colonial Era*

*Petitions and Judgments Cecil County Court, 1717–1732:
Abstracts with Selected Transcriptions*

International Standard Book Number
Paperbound: 978-1-55613-163-9

June Court 1724

At a Court of the Right Honourable Charles
Absolute Lord and Proprietary of the Provinces of Maryland
and Avalon Lord Baron of Baltimore &c held for Cecil county
at the Court house on Sd River the Ninth day of June in the
Tenth year of his Said Lordship's Dominion &c Anno domini 1724
and there Continued untill the Eleventh day of the Same month
by his Said Lordship's Justices and other Officer authorized &
appointed to hold the same Court of whome were

The Worshipfull

Mr. John Inwert   Coll Benj Pearce
Maj Francis Maulden   Mr Peter Jackson
Esq James Alexander   Mr Rich Thompson   Present

Mr Henry Ward

John Hack Sheriff.   Step Knight Clk

Read the Petition of John Hack &c

To The Worshipfull the Justices of Cecil County.
The Humble Petition of John Hack sheweth
That your Petitioner having in his Custody a Certain
Person Dutch who is Condemned to be hang'd within the ninth
day of this Instant June and your Petitioner being fear
full thro the Insufficiency of Goal humbly requisite
your Worships order to provide a Sufficient standing Goal
in Order to secure the said Prisoner till he is brought
to Condign Punishment and that your Petitioner
performance be usuall as allowed to the Sheriff both
of this and the Neighbouring Government as also
in Order to summons the Constables of the severall hund
reds of the said County to be at your Petitioner Goal &

Folio 63 (Image DSC02200), Petitions and Judgments, Cecil County
Court.

Introduction

Sometime in the 1990s two original volumes of Cecil County court records were donated to the Historical Society of Cecil County (HSCC) by a person whose name is now lost from the Society's records. The prior history of these volumes is unknown, but they were no doubt among the records confiscated by the British Army under General Howe when it passed through Elkton during its campaign to capture Philadelphia in August 1777. (See Johnston's *History of Cecil County*, p.333.) Nothing is known about their disposition in the intermediate years.

The two volumes differ in their content. The older volume, referred to as Volume 1, covers the period 1702 to 1717 and contains records of the full range of judicial proceedings, including crimes, lawsuits and the justices' administrative decisions. Volume 2, which covers the period 1717 to 1732, contains only formal petitions made by individuals or groups and the court's decision in each case. The present work contains abstracts from the second volume. It was produced working from the digital copy of the original volume located at the HSCC. The location of each entry in this work is identified by both the folio (f) number from the original volume and the DSC number of the digital image on which it appears in the society's digital copy.

The court usually met in four sessions during the year—April, June, August and November—beginning on the second Tuesday of the month and lasting three to five days. There were typically five to eight justices sitting on the "bench," all appointed by the provincial governor. The particular individuals varied little from session to session, but occasional changes occurred as new members were appointed and older ones withdrew. The county sheriff and clerk were also always present.

These records provide a fascinating glimpse into the lives and concerns of our colonial predecessors in early 18th century Cecil County. A wide spectrum of public and private matters ranging from petty to routine to momentous came before the court for its consideration and judgment. This was a period when the county's basic infrastructure and organization were just being established. Many petitions concern the establishment or rerouting of paths and roads, the operation of ferries and the licensing of public houses for the convenience of commerce and travelers. Common cases concerned such things as indenture disputes and requests for tax relief or simple charity by indigents no longer able to support themselves. Perhaps the most frequent petitions were for the formation of a commission to investigate the boundaries of a property whose corner markers had eroded or disappeared over time. Also mentioned in the records is the relocation of the Courthouse from Sassafras to Elkton in 1719.

This work includes abstracts of all court actions recorded in Volume 2. Every name mentioned in these actions is cited in the abstracts. In addition, a collection of full transcriptions of selected actions has been compiled in the Addendum. They were chosen as representative vignettes to capture and convey the personalities and milieu of colonial Cecil County in their own original words.

Public distribution of this work is restricted to printed copies. A digital copy has been made available to the Historical Society of Cecil County. Volunteers may assist patrons in researching specific items there, or in downloading selected, limited portions of the text in digital form.

The author would especially like to thank Ms. Emily Kilby of Fair Hill, Cecil County, for her very helpful editing of this book.

John F. Polk, Ph.D.
January 2021

Petitions and Judgments
Cecil County Court
1717-1732

The original folios of the court record were not numbered, but sequential folio (f) numbers were penciled in at a later date on some folios. The DSC number identifies the digital image of the folio as presently stored in the electronic-image files at the HSCC.

An asterisk * following the petition heading indicates that a full transcript will be found in the Addendum.

f.0 (DSC02169)
==

March Court 1717
Court convened 11 March 1717 at Sassafras, continued until 15 March.*
Following commissioners present: Matthias Van Bebber, Ephraim Augustine Herman, John Ward, Stephen Knight, Guning Bedford, John Jawart. Also present, John Dowdall, Clerk.

Petition of James Heath. 4 March 1717. States that his land lies in both Cecil and Kent Counties but he has always lived and paid taxes in Cecil. Heretofore he has taken his tobacco to south side of Head of Sassafras in Kent County, but the carting and rolling road was recently altered so he can no longer use it. Asks that a new rolling and carting road be laid out in Cecil from his plantation to the landing at Head of Sassafras in Cecil County. Court agrees and appoints Col. John Ward and Stephen Knight to lay out a new road and directs that inhabitants along the way who might benefit to assist in the clearing and construction of the road.

3

Note at bottom of folio: "Recorded this 13th day of July 1722. Stephen Knight, Clk. Cecil County"
f.1 (DSC02169)

===

March Court 1718
Court convened 10 March 1718 at Sassafras, continued until 15 March. Following commissioners present: Matthias Van Bebber, John Jewart, Francis Mauldin, Guning Bedford.

Petition of Benjamin Pearce. States that the main road by his home is inconvenient to travelers and injurious to him. Asks that the road be turned from the mill to Charles Mullins plantation and thence to the main road. Granted.

Petition of John Brannock. Rejected.

Petition of Clem Barkston. Rejected.

Petition of James Gallaway.* Complains about his servant Mary Emerson who has had two "base born" children and brought scandal to his house. Asks court for damages. Court orders that Mary Emerson serve nine months beyond her contracted indenture.

f.2 (DSC02170)

===

Court adjourned until 3rd Monday in April.

Court convenes 20 April.

Petition of James Frisby and Peregrine Frisby. States that they have an action pending in court on account of their brother Thomas and a similar action in provincial court. Asks that their case be postponed until following session as they cannot be in both places. Granted.

Petition of Clement Barkston. Asks court for license to keep a "house of entertainment" at Bohemia River ferry. Court approved subject to compliance with laws.

4

June Court 1719

Court convened 9 June 1719. Following commissioners present: Matthias Van Bebber, Francis Mauldin, Matthias Vanderheyden, Col. John Ward, Col. Ephraim Augustine Herman.

f.3 (DSC02170)
==

Petition of Robert Gibbs, late of Newcastle County. Testifies concerning Ann, widow of Thomas Horne, now Gibbs's wife, and her son Robert. States that she sometimes had fits of near madness and, in his absence while away working, had been taken advantage of while in a fit by a Robert Hodgson, alias Hutchison, and "put her hand to a sham indenture" making her son Robert a servant to Hodgson. The agreement was apparently sold to a merchant named White for £5 but they had since reimbursed White and have now placed Robert as an apprentice to James Alexander of New Munster, tanner. Asks court to make a judgment on the matter, mentioning Thomas Boone as a witness who would verify his account. Granted.
(Note: The foregoing text is particularly difficult to read and make sense of.)

f.4 (DSC02171)
==

Petition of Sarah Price (Prue). Pleads that she is old and a destitute widow suffering from many ailments and diseases of the body. Asks for support from the county. Court allows her 1,000 lbs/tbco from next levy in November.

Petition of Mary Othoson.* Notes that the County Court has relocated from Sassafras (to Elkton) and that the former courthouse is no longer needed and the county wishes to dispose of it. She asks that she have rights to sale or refusal thereof. Granted.

Petition of Mary Hendrick. Rejected

Petition of Simon Johnson. Rejected.

5

August Court 1719

Court convened 2nd Tuesday in August 1719. Following commissioners present: Matthias Van Bebber, Francis Mauldin, Matthias Vanderheyden, Mr. Gunning Bedford, Mr. John Jawert.

f.5 (DSC02171)

===

Petition of David McBride. States that he has applied himself to studying the law and asks to be admitted as an attorney to the court. Court approves subject to his taking the oath of an attorney and subscribe as directed.

Petition of William Brastow (Bristow). Rejected.

Petition of Henry Slyter and Samuel Bayard. Makes requests concerning mill at head of Bohemia River. [Very hard to decipher the specific request.] Granted.

Petition of Clement Barkston. Notes that John Simons will leave the Bohemia River ferry in November and asks that he, Barkston, be given agency for it with whatever allowance they may be pleased to grant. Granted.

Petition of Abell Barkuloo. Notes that there are not attorneys in court to assist him or other persons who "have need to make use of the law." Asks that he be allowed to represent himself and other persons who think fit to use his services. Granted, "he qualifying himself according to laws."

f.6 (DSC02172)

===

November Court 1719

Court convened 10 November 1719. Following commissioners present: Matthias Van Bebber, Col. John Ward, Mr. Francis Mauldin, Col. Eph. Aug. Herman, Mr. John Jawert.

Petition of several inhabitants of Susquehanna Hundred.* States that they are settled in a remote area and "destitute of a convenient road both to church and Court and alsoe for rowling tobacco to a convenient landing." Ask the court to order a road be laid out from the head of the river to the plantation of Roger Kerk. Signed by ___ Patton, Samuel Price, Enoch Enochson, Jonathan Jones, Samuel Bowen, John Noland(?), Esten(?) Brown, John Darlington, James Morriss, Jonas Moonn, Nath. Baker, Henry Bowen, James Allmond, Roger Kerk, Barnat Rosenbein(?), Samuel Harris, William Lee, James Bond, Robert Hand, ___ Benett. Granted.

Petition of Robert Oldham. Rejected.

Petition of Ebenezer Cook.* States that he has practiced law in several courts and asks to be admitted to Cecil Court. Granted, "he qualifying himself according to law, which he doth."

f.7 (DSC02172)
==
Petition of the northern inhabitants of the county. States that a road is needed "leading from ___ or further north if need requires into the road from Henry Hollingsworth's to the landing and alsoe a road leading from the said ___ to the Great Branch of Elk River where the New Munster road intersects the same and a road leading from [where] is most convenient from said road to the Courthouse for the said inhabitants. As also a Church Road at the head of North East ___. " Signed Robert Hodgson, John Hollingsworth, Joseph Hollingsworth, John Smith, Henry Hollingsworth, Thomas Phillips, Joseph Carter. Granted.

Petition of George Robinson. Rejected.

Petition of John Simmons. Asks court to grant his wages for keeping the ferry over Bohemia River for the year. Granted. No amount specified.

Petition of Clem. Barkston: Rejected.

Petition of William Jones.* States that he has a license to keep a public house at his dwelling plantation but that it is remote from the courthouse. Asks to build a house near the courthouse for "entertaining your Worships and sev'll sutors to this Court." Granted, "he complying with the laws in such cases made."

f.8 (DSC02173)

==

Petition of Jacob Archer. States that he lives at a place of public trade which is "opprest with travelers and others." Requests he be given a license for a house of entertainment. Granted.

Petition of Clem Barkston. States that he had the grant for the ferry over Bohemia River but from sundry misfortunes was not prepared for it as was expected. Asks court a reasonable price as they think fit to buy a boat that he will have ready for them to see if they grant him eight or 10 days. Granted.

Petition of Aron Lathom. Asks court for a lot on the courthouse lane where he may build a house for lodging people during court sessions or other times as needed. Court considers the petition. No decision stated.

Petition of Roger Larramore.* States that he has an old negro woman who is both lame and blind and wholly incapable of maintaining herself. Asks that court make her levy free. Granted.

f.9 (DSC02173)

==

Petition of Jeremiah Lukins. Rejected.

Petition of Thomas Burgey. Rejected.

Petition of Herman Kuckey. Rejected.

Record of sale of old courthouse at Sassafras.* Court orders Commissioners Matthias Van Bebber, Col. John Ward and John Jawert to meet at the old courthouse at Sassafras on 9 February to conduct an auction of the building and grounds. Bids are to be made in increments of at least 100 lbs/tbco, and the winning bidder is to post security with the sheriff. Minimum bid: 2,000 lbs/tbco. Auction was held, with Col. John Ward being the highest bidder at 5,700 lbs/tbco. Court awards Ward the house and land.

Court adjourned until March session.

March Court 1719

Court convened 10 November 1719 at Elk River. Following commissioners present: Matthias Van Bebber, Col. Eph. Aug. Herman, Mr. Francis Mauldin, Mr. Gunning Bedford, Mr. John Jawert.

f.10 (DSC02174)
===

Petition of Mary Hendrickham.* States that her husband, John Hendrickham, refuses without reason to provide any allowance for the maintenance of herself and child. Asks court to take "such methods" as needed so that "neither the petitioner nor child may be subject to misery through the unlawful and inhumane dealings of my husband." Justices issue summons for John Hendrickham's immediate appearance in court. Henrickham appears and petition is read again. Court orders that John Hendrickson pay all fees due his wife, "having been prosecuted for suspicion of bigamy."

Petition of William Jeenes. Rejected.

Petition of Hugh Morris. Rejected.

Petition of Thomas Smith. States that the main road by his plantation is "somewhat crooked and out of the way." Asks permission to clear another path that would be "a nearer and better road for all travellers." Petition granted.

Petition of Charles Mullins. Postponed.

f.11 (DSC02174)
===

Petition of John Currer.* States that he had been summoned for jury duty by William Dare, deputy to Sheriff Abell Barkeloo and was "fully resolved" to appear but a few days before "it pleased God to afflict ____ " [page obliterated; probably refers to his father or son] who died on the day Currer was to be in court. He was apparently fined 500 lbs/tbco for his nonappearance. Asks court to "remit" his fine. The matter was "duly considered by the Court," but no decision is recorded.

Court adjourned until June session.

June Court 1720. None of the justices of the quorum appearing, the court was dismissed.

August Court 1720
Court convened 9 August 1720 at Elk River.* Following commissioners present: Mr. John Dowdall, Mr. Benjamin Pearce, Mr. William Dare, Mr. Richard Thompson, Mr. Roger Larramore, Mr. Edward Jackson.

Petition of Edward Gunning. No further information.

Petition of Henry Worley. Rejected.

f.12 (DSC02175)
===

November Court 1720
Court convened __ November 1720 at Elk River. Following commissioners present: Col. Eph. Aug. Herman, Mr. William Dare, Mr. John Dowdall, Mr. Benjamin Pearce, Mr. Roger Larramore, Mr. Edward Jackson, Mr. Richard Thompson.

Petition of Joseph Presberry. States that he had been "concerned" in the sheriff's and other offices in Baltimore County and asks that he be admitted to practice in Cecil Court. Granted.

Petition of diverse inhabitants of Milford Hundred. Refers to petition approved by court the previous fall to have four roads laid out in their area of which three were done. Petitioners state that they cannot find suitable land for the fourth and ask court's approval to drop it. Signed by _____ Rees, Alexander White, Morgan Patton, Isaac Miller, William _____, Adam Short, John Thomas, David Payne, Thomas Ricketts, Griffith Nichols, Samuel Wild, James Mafett, Abraham Hollingsworth, Rowland Chambers,

James _____, Andrew Wallace, James Seth, Thomas Sharp. Petition granted.

Petition of Henry Worley. States that he is settled on the main road at head of Northeast Creek and is often asked by travelers for meat, drink and lodgings which he cannot legally sell without a license. Text is hard to read but Worley appears to be asking for a license to keep an ordinary. Granted.

f.13 (DSC02175)
==
Petition of Ralph Rutter. States that he has been a taxable for some 50 years in the county but is now "worn out with age and disabled in the shoulder." Asks that he be exempted from the levy. Court approves and grants Rutter 350 lbs/tbco.

Petition of William Garriss. No description of his situation. Court orders he be allowed 1,200 lbs/tbco from next levy for his clothing and maintenance.

Petition of Rowland Chambers and Stephen Hollingsworth. Rejected.

Petition of James Gallway. States that he was ordered to take a mulatto boy into his house from June to August Court, for which he would be compensated. States that he has kept the boy through November and asks for payment. Court allows him 450 lbs/tbco.

f.14 (DSC02176)
==
Petition of Elenor Collins.* States that years ago a certain Thomas Heaptharp, an orphan in her care, was by order of the court made an apprentice of Thomas Rogers to learn a cooper's trade and to read and write. Collins complains that Rogers has failed to do as obliged, instead compelling the boy to work daily with ax and hoe. Asks the court to consider the situation and render justice on Heaptharp's behalf. Court issues summons for Rogers and the orphan boy to be brought into court. After hearing the case court grants the petition and orders the boy returned to Collins.

11

March Court 1720

Court convened 2nd Tuesday March 1720 at Elk River. Following commissioners present: Mr. Matthias Van Bebber, Mr. Edward Jackson, Mr. John Jawert, Mr. Richard Thompson, Mr. Samuel Alexander, Maj. Dowdall, Richard Thompson.

f.15 (DSC02176)

==

Petition of Lewis Jones. States that a road has been cut through his land from New Munster to head of Elk and that he had not been informed in advance. States that the road may be made straighter and better along a different route and asks court's approval to make changes. Plot of the proposed modification is included in the record. Court directs Henry Hollingsworth to inspect the alternative routes. He reports back that the proposed road is as good as the former road. Court grants the petition, Jones to cover the cost and charges for the new route.

Petition of Thomas Manswell/Mansell. States that Owen McGragh, in his last sickness, made Manswell and Dr. Matthew executors and had declared that he wished Manswell to care for his son John, which he now does. Petition mentions that the parents were Roman Catholic, which he presumes will not present a problem, and states that the child is six years old. Asks court to appoint him as guardian and promises to teach him how to read, write and do cost accounts. Court grants petition.

f.16 (DSC02177)

==

Petition of Alexander Meaver. States he lives by main road leading from upper part of county to Sassafras ferry. Asks to be allowed to keep a house of entertainment. Granted.

Petition of John Morriss. Rejected.

Petition of Hugh Jones. Rejected.

Petition of Jacob Archer. Rejected.

Petition of Thomas Pope. States he lives by the ferry point, not named, and is much troubled with travelers. Asks that court to permit him to keep a public house that he "may turn a penny." Granted.

f.17 (DSC02177)
===
Petition of Richard Dobson, constable of Susquehanna Hundred. States that he will be moving out of the hundred and asks to be discharged of responsibilities. Suggests that Henry Webb and William Currer be appointed. Court directs same be granted.

Petition of Aron Latham.* States that he had purchased three lots near the courthouse that had been laid out by Commissioner [John] Jawart pursuant to direction of the court. He built a small house on one, but now asks court to allow him to swap his two remaining lots for a lot by the river where no other houses are yet built. He proposes to build a larger house for entertainment of travelers. The new location would pose no fire hazard to Mr. Jones' house near the original lots. Court agrees.

f.18 (DCS02178)
===
Petition of Catherine Hanson. States that she now lives in "a great resort of trade partly occasioned by her trade or occupation" and at times has much trouble. Neither occupation nor location is identified. Asks for permission to keep an ordinary. Granted.

Court adjourned until June session.

June Court 1721
Court convened 2nd Tuesday, 13 June 1721 at Elk River. Following commissioners present: Mr. Matthias Van Bebber, Mr. Richard Thompson, Mr. John Jawert, Mr. Edward Jackson, Mr. Samuel Alexander, Mr. Benjamin Pearce, Mr. William Dare.

Petition of Mr. William Vanhaesdunke Ridlesden. Rejected.

Petition of Daniel Benson. Rejected.

Petition of the inhabitants of New Munster.* Refers to earlier direction of the court permitting a road to be built from the main road near Thomas Jacobs to New Munster, seven miles long, which they say was quickly and well built to the satisfaction of neighboring persons. They complain that road is now being obstructed by Lewis Jones and accomplices who have redirected it in a way that is much longer and more hazardous. Jones apparently claims the existing road causes problems to his property. Petitioners respond that many others can make same objection. Signed by James Alexander, John Gillespie, Gavin Roper(?), David Alexander, Arthur Alexander, John Wallas [Wallace], James McClure, James Alexander, Phillip Davis, Peter Highgate, James Alexander. Court directs that "the road stand as it was formerly."

f.19 (DCS02178)

==
Petition of Richard Parsley. States that when George Cuzine died he left two young sons whom Parsley has raised since marrying Cuzine's widow. The two sons, now aged 13 and 16, have lately been taken into the houses of other unknown persons. Asks court to bind the two sons to him or other good person to learn a trade. Court issues a summons for Melissa Hyland and John Pennington to bring George Cuzine's children to court.

f.20 (DSC02179)

==
Petition of John Hollet.* States that he is the "reputative" father of a boy named John Hollett, now aged about 13, the son of Sarah Kerres. Said boy was bound by the court since infancy to a certain Paul Allen who in now dead, as is his wife. The boy is now being kept by James Collins with no legal authority. Asks that the court bind the boy over to him until age 21 since "nobody has a more visible right concerning him than your petitioner." Court agrees and directs that the boy be delivered to Hollet.

Petition of Jane Francklin. Complains that she has kept the child of Lawrence Lawrenceson for 15 months but Lawrenceson refuses to pay for same. Asks court to compel payment. Court grants petition. No amount stated.

Court adjourned until August session.

August Court 1721

Court convened 8 August 1721 at Elk River. Following commissioners present: Mr. Matthias Van Bebber, Mr. Richard Thompson, Mr. Edward Jackson, Mr. John Jawert, Mr. Samuel Alexander, Mr. Benjamin Pearce, Mr. James Alexander.

f.21 (DSC02179)
==

Petition of David McBride. Rejected.

Petition of John and Rebecca Simmons. Rejected.

Petition of Caslevew(?). Rejected.

Petition of William Van Riddlesden. Refers to prior session at which he petitioned court to be admitted to practice in the court, but the decision was postponed. Asks that he be admitted at this time. Granted.

Petition of Henry Hollingsworth. States that he had served on previous Orphan's Jury but did not appear on the second day and was fined. States that his nonappearance was caused by a meeting with "his Excellency Governour." Asks that his fine be remitted. Granted.

Petition of Henry Hollingsworth (appended to foregoing). Rejected.

Petition of William Howell. States that he had for some time worked with the sheriff's office and has been studying the laws of Great Britain and of the province. Requests that he be admitted as an attorney to the court. Granted.

f.22(DSC02180)
==

November Court 1721

Court convened 14 November 1721 at Elk River.* Following commissioners present: Mr. John Jawert, Mr. James Alexander, Mr. Edward Jackson, Mr. Benjamin Pearce, Mr. Francis Mauldin, Mr. Samuel Alexander.

Petition of Clement Barkston. Requests payment of 5,000 lbs/tbco for keeping the Bohemia ferry the past year, as provided by the court; also asks that he be permitted to keep the ferry again for the ensuing year. Further states that whoever keeps the ferry will have to pay Lord Baltimore £4 "current silver money of Maryland" and requests that an equivalent amount be added to the keeper's wages. Court grants petition, "he having the usual allowances in that case made and provided."

Petition of inhabitants of Milford Hundred. Rejected.

Petition of John Stocke. Rejected.

Petition of Ben Mason. Postponed.

Petition of William Garriss(?). Asks for support from the county, not being able to support himself or come to court. Court allows him 1,200 lbs/tbco.

Petition of John Jawart. Postponed.

f.23 (DSC02180)
===
Petition of James Campbell. States that he has been granted a commission from "the honourable Bennett Lowe, Esq." to keep ferry at Susquehanna. Requests a license from county to keep a house of entertainment. Granted.

Petition of Ralph Rutter. States that he is too old to work and has no estate on which to subsist or pay his levy. Asks that he be made exempt of the levy and be given some allowance by the county. Court grants petition and allows Rutter 250 lbs/tbco.

Petition of George Dowglass. Postponed.

Petition of Rowland Chambers & Stephen Hollingsworth. Rejected.

Petition of New Munster inhabitants. Rejected.

Petition of John Simmons. Rejected.

Petition of John Brown. States that he is disabled by age and other infirmities and asks for some support from the county. Court allows him 150 lbs/tbco from next levy.

f.24 (DSC02181)
==
Petition of John Ham.* States that he stood as godfather to Evan Lewis, son of Edward Lewis, in a baptism done in the rites of the Church of England. Edward Lewis is now deceased, and Evan Lewis is kept among Roman Catholics "contrary to the intention of his Baptism." Ham therefore asks court to have the child removed and placed with another family where he will be brought up in the faith of the Church of England. Court agrees and orders that Mary Lewis, wife of Edward Lewis, bring her "son in law," Evan Lewis, into court.

Petition of William Rumsey. Asks court for 600 lbs/tbco in payment for his work ordered by them, including transcription of "rules of the Court" and five days' attendance at court. Granted. 300 lbs/tbco to be raised from current public levy.

Petition of Benjamin Davis. Requests that court appoint him to care for his two brothers, Maurice and William Davis, until they be of age. Granted.

f.25 (DSC02181)
==
Petition of Henry Hendrickson.* States that he had cared for Cane Allen who was disabled and has died. Requests court pay his expenses. Court allows Hendrickson 30 lbs/tbco for cost of crutches and 200 lbs/tbco for cost of Allen's coffin.

Petition of some citizens of Cecil County as subscribed.* States that the Elk River ferry was being maintained by negroes without oversight by their master and were negligent in their duties. Also states that the nearby land of Herman Kinkey was impaired by the roads leading to the ferry, making it hard to cultivate. Requests court put Kinkey in charge of maintaining the ferry. Signed by Robert Dutton, Thomas Hichcock, Alexander Meceny, Ralph Rutter, Gunning Bedford, William Currer, Darby Wheelding, Joseph Hollingsworth, Henry Denning, Peter Mannadow, Rick Forster, William Howell, Henrey Starr, John Carsy, Evan ____, Morgan Patten, David Wallace, Lewis Griffith, John Bower, John Thomas, John Sim(mons) Richard Dobson, William and Francis Jenkins, John Underhill, John Carer, Joseph Young, James Allmond, William Corer, Ralph Bowen, Johanna Hanberson, Daniell Hukill, John Gray, William Husband, Gabriell Clement, John Hans ____, William Sinclair, Henry Pennington, John Roberts, Math Mathiason, James Hu____, Robert Dullon, Thomas Hichcock, James Alexander, Benjamin Cox, Thomas Peirce, William Forster, John Court, Thomas Johnson, John Sartill, Jarack Horsey. Rejected.

f.26 (DSC92182)

===
Petition of some citizens of Cecil County.* States that the great road leading "over the dangerous and swelling falls of the two heads of Elk River" is dangerous and inconvenient. Requests court to have "horse and foot" bridges built over said falls. Signed by Roger Merick, Richard Rutter, Thomas Beettle, Robert Eyre, Henry Reynolds, John Smith, Gavin Hutcheson, Richard Tatcher, Richard Dobson, William Forster, Hugh Lawson, David Reece, John Jones, Thomas Jacobs, Henry Hollingsworth, Rowland Chambers, Joseph Hollingsworth, Adam Hollingsworth, Renece Vancole, George Robinson, Zebulon Hollingsworth, John Thomas, Isaiah Phipps, Martin Cartmell, Stephen Hollingsworth, Martin Alexander, William Bristow, Richard Fredey. Granted.

March Court 1721
Court convened 13 March 1721 at Elk River, continued to 17 March. Following commissioners present: John Jawert, James Alexander, Francis Mauldin, Benjamin Pearce, Samuel Alexander, Edward Jackson.

Petition of John Roland, Jun. Rejected

Petition of Mssrs Briggs and Warner. Postponed until next November Court.

f.27 (DSC92182)

==

Petition of William Carper.* States that he had served William Price of Cecil for six years and three months and agreed to pay Price 20 shillings for the three months remaining of his indenture. Carper claims he made the final payment of 10 shillings on the agreed-upon day, but William Price refused to sign a discharge of his indenture. Instead he caused Carper to be apprehended as a runaway, then sold his services to John Veazey. Carper states that Price coerced him into signing a two-year indenture with Veazey and requests court to relieve him of same. Court orders Carper to serve Veazey according to the indenture.

f.28 (DSC02183)

==

Petition of inhabitants and freeholders of Cecil.* (Clerk notes that this was filed in November Court but was omitted from the record so is entered at this time. Petition dated 14 Nov 1721.) Petitioners state that James Van Bebber former sheriff of Cecil unlawfully took 8,601 lbs/tbco from them for the levy and had been indicted by the grand jury for so doing, but that the indictment had not been brought because of "some colour of friendship, relation or otherwise." Request that Van Bebber be brought before the court and the matter be prosecuted. Signed James Alexander, Evan Reece, John Ward, A Burkeloo, James Creagar, John Roberts, Hugh Matthews, Richard Thompson, James Husbands, William Chick, Ephm Aug. Herman, George Douglas, Matt Matthiason, John Smith, John Hollett, William Veazey, William Husbands, Benjamin Cox, Robert Penington, Thomas Pearce, William Price, Jun., Henry Penington, Richard Dobson, John Dowdall, Thomas Mareer, John Ham, John Thomas, Henry Ward, John Numbers, Henry Penington, Jun., Joseph Hollingsworth, William Penington, John Campbell, Nicholas Dorrele, Alexander Macay, Albert Cox, John Simonds, Aaron Latham, Thomas Pope, William Bristow, Thomas Johnson, Peter Picott, James Veazey, John Marly, Joseph Lillifre, Richard Whitton, Walter Scott, Robert Hodgson, Daniel Huckele, Corn. Eliason, Henry Hendrickson, Francis Steel, Thomas Croger. Court considered the matter and postponed for an hour. James Van Bebber appeared in court and promised to pay the claimed amount of tobacco which court orders to be put into the present levy.

===

June Court 1722

Court convened 2nd Tuesday, 12 June 1722 at Elk River, continued to 16 June. Following commissioners present: Mr. Matthias Van Bebber, Col. Benjamin Pearce, John Jawert, Mr. Samuel Alexander, Mr. Francis Mauldin, Mr. James Alexander, Mr. Edward Jackson.

Petition of Joshua George.* States that he had practiced in the chancery and provincial courts and several other courts in the province. Request to be admitted as an attorney in Cecil County Court. Court approves. George takes usual oaths and signs "the Oath of Abjuration and the Test, etc. according to the law."

Petition of Allexander Frazer. Asks to be admitted as an attorney of the court. Granted. Frazer takes the usual oaths and the Oath of Abjuration and signs "The Test, etc as the Law directs."

Petition of Samuel Brice.* States that he has been a resident of and paid taxes in Cecil County for some time but that the surveyor of Chester County had on 11 March surveyed land adjacent to his and rendered it "inconvenient," to his detriment. Also states that other neighbors, Daniel Smith, George Sluyter, James Bond, Edward Long, John Allen, Charles Allen and several others were complying with the Pennsylvania survey and titles although they had for some time considered themselves inhabitants of Cecil County. Brice "loudly calls for redress." Court directs sheriff "to bring the body of Isaac Taylor Surveyor of Chester County aforesaid and all the other persons concerned in the breach of the peace in the said petition" into court.

f.30 (DSC 02184)

===

Court "adjourns till to Morrow morn, 8 a clock."

Petition of Lidia Hollingsworth. States that an orphan girl named Catherine Lancaster had previously lived with Henry Roberts but is now staying with her. Hollingsworth requests to be appointed mistress of Lancaster and promises to perform whatever is required by law in such cases. Court approves.

Petition of Elizabeth Sluyter.* States that her father is lately deceased and that she is now of age to choose her guardian. Requests that court appoint her brother Benjamin Sluyter as her guardian. Court approves.

f.31 (DSC 02184)

==

Petition of Elizabeth Clements, wife of Michael Clements. States that her husband has sold all his personal and real estate and is "not to be entrusted on his account." She says she is exposed "under the circumstances to be chargeable to her friends etc." Asks court to intercede. Court orders Michael Clement to appear at next court "to be further examined and proceeded against in relation to the said Petition."

Petition of William Bristow. States that he is godfather of the only son of Edward Luis, now deceased. The boy has been "left with a grevious sore legg and no effects or anything vissabell for the boys cure or sustainment." Asks court to provide some assistance. Court allows "all reasonable charges" towards a cure of the boy's affliction.

Court adjourned and reconvened 10 o'clock next day (Thursday, 14 March). Same commissioners.

f.32 (DSC02185)

==

Petition of William Sinclear.* States that he has maintained an orphan, George Lancaster, son of his sister, and provided him schooling. Lancaster is now 14 at which age he can choose his guardian. Sinclear says he is willing to continue caring for the orphan but asks court to decide and appoint a guardian. Court appoints Sinclear as guardian to Lancaster.

Court adjourned and reconvened 9:00 next day (Friday 15 March). No actions recorded.

Court adjourned and reconvened 8:00 next day (Saturday, 16 March). Same commissioners.

Petition of John Copen. States that court had appointed him to care for the child of a certain Ann Cookeey who has since married and now wishes to care for the child herself. Copen is agreeable and asks court to relieve him of any responsibilities. Court agrees and declares all previous covenants with Copen to be void and that Ann Cookeey and her husband are to assume care of the child.

Court adjourned until August session.

f.33 (DSC02185)
==

August Court 1722
Court convened 2nd Tuesday, 14 August 1722 at Elk River, continued to 17 August. Following commissioners present: John Jawert, Mr. Samuel Alexander, Mr. Francis Mauldin, Mr. James Alexander, Mr. Edward Jackson. Also present John Hack, sheriff, and Stephen Knight, clerk.

Petition of Thomas Pope. States that he keeps a public house but had committed some irregularities for which the court had suspended his business. He thanks court for not having taken more drastic action and asks that he be allowed to keep his public house as before; promises not to give them any cause for complaint. Granted.

Court adjourned and reconvened on 15th August.

Petition of Joseph Steale [Steel]. States that a road going from the northern part of the county to Head of Elk runs through his property but is little used and causes him many problems. Asks permission to reroute the road on good ground. Court approves.

f.34 (DSC02186)
==
Petition of Jacob Archer.* Provides an account about his servant Hugh Morris who ran away for 11 days. Van Bebber incurred costs for having him returned and asks court for redress of costs. Court orders that Morris serve an extra 200 days on his indenture.

Court adjourned and reconvened on 16 August.

Petition of Jacob Watts. Rejected.

Petition of James Bull, a minor. Court appoints Francis Mauldin as guardian for Bull.

Court adjourned and reconvened on 17 August

Petition of Robert Willson.* States that he was held in the common prison of the county by Mathias Van Bebber on suspicion of being a runaway. Further states that no one has come forth to make claim on him or charged him with any crimes. Asks that he be discharged from sheriff's custody. Granted.

Petition of John Campbell. Campbell provides an account against Edward Bannister and Anthony Whitley for six days of runaway time plus £7/2/10 in costs for having them returned, Court orders they each serve 3½ months additional to their indenture obligations.

f.35 (DSC02186)
==
Petition of Elizabeth Jones. States that she has served "the accustomed years appointed in this province for orphans of our sex to serve." She is now destitute and afflicted by some malady and begs some assistance from the court. Court appoints Adam Wallace to care for her until November court and to be provided allowance for same.

Court adjourned until November session.

November Court 1722

Court convened 2nd Tuesday, 13 November 1722 at Elk River, continued to 17 November. Following commissioners present: Mr. Matthias Van Bebber, Mr. Samuel Alexander, Mr. John Jawart, Mr. James Alexander, Mr. Edward Jackson. Also present John Hack, sheriff, and Stephen Knight, clerk. Commission of Oyer and Terminer read in court. Justices take the oaths and subscribe the Oath of Abjuration and the Test.

Court adjourned and reconvened Wednesday 14 November.
f.36 (DSC02187)

===

Petition of Bartholemew Johnson.* States that a traveler was found on main road near his house by Adam Wallace and Johnson's wife. The said traveler was mute and sick. Johnson and his family took the man in and cared for him but he died in their house. They provided a decent burial for him and now ask for some allowance from the county for his expenses. Court allows him 400 lbs/tbco from next levy.

Petition of Thomas Oldham. Postponed.

Petition of Ralph Rutter. States that he, being old and "past his labour," has been levy free for some years. Requests that he continue to be levy free. Court approves and allows petitioner 200 lbs/tbco from present levy.

Petition of Herman Kinkey. Postponed

Col. Henry Ward joins Court. Col. Ward is one of the justices appointed for the commission of Oyer and Terminer. He takes usual oaths and the Oath of Abjuration and the Test, then takes his seat.

Petition of Clement Barkston. Postponed

Petition of John Hack. Postponed.

Allowance for John Glenn(?). Court allows John Glenn 200 lbs/tbco from present levy.

Court adjourned and reconvened 15 November 1722.

Petition of Clement Barkston. Has kept Bohemia ferry for past year for 5,000 lbs/tbco. Requests that this be renewed and that some provision be made to cover the cost for the high license fee paid to Lord Baltimore. Court agrees to continue Barkston as ferry keeper and allows 5,000 lbs/tbco but rejects request for additional funds.

f.37 (DSC02187)

==

Petition of John Hack. States that he lives near the Bohemia public ferry and notes "there have been so many just complaints against the present ferry man." Requests he be allowed to keep the ferry, promising he will have two boats and it will be well kept. Court approves and allows 5,000 lbs/tbco for keeping the service until next November.

Petition of Clement Barkston. Asks that he may be discharged of his recognizances for keeping a public house. Granted.

Petition of William Beaston. States that he lives by the unspecified main road and is bothered by many people passing by. Requests "the liberty to sell a cup of liquor to those that may have occasion for the same." Court grants him approval to keep a public house where he now lives.

f.38 (DSC02188)

==

Court adjourned and reconvened Friday 16 November.

Petition of George Robinson. States that he contributed 212 lbs/tbco to the 1718 levy which was not his duty to pay. Asks that he be credited for it in the current levy. Granted.

Petition of William Howell. States that he had been directed by the court to bring Mr. Isaac Taylor (Chester County surveyor) into court, which he did at his expense and asks to be paid for his services. Court allows him 240 lbs/tbco.

f.39 (DSC02188)

==

Petition of Martha Mounts. States that she has been taking care of William Garish, a cripple, for the county for three or four years but he is now so incapacitated that he can do nothing for himself and requires constant attention. Furthers states that she has received nothing from the county in past year but was wholly omitted from the levy. Court orders that she be allowed 2,400 lbs/tbco from present levy for keeping Garish for two years.

Petition of Joseph Hollingsworth. States that he was supervisor of the highways the past year, served on the petite jury last June and also on present jury and now is deputed as a constable. Asks that he be relieved of constable duties. Court concurs and appoints Jonathan Curtis as constable in the place of Lewis Jones instead of Hollingsworth.

Petition of Peter Bayard. Postponed.

Petition of William Rumsey on behalf of estate of William Dare. Estate is allowed 375 lbs/tbco.

Petition of William Howell, clerk of North Elk Parish.* Requests support from the county for sundry expense of the church, as the Act of Assembly provides. Court allows 10 lbs/tbco per parishioner in present levy.

f.40 (DSC02189)
==
Allowance for Sarah Price [Prue]. Being a poor distressed woman is allowed 1,500 lbs/tbco from present levy.

Petition of Peter Bayard. Postponed.

Petition of John Jawart. States he had been a ferryman at Elk River for the county since it was settled. Asks that he may be continued with the former, unspecified allowance. Court directs that he be granted allowance for the past year but rejects petition to continue him for next year.

Petition of John Thomas.* States that he has built two bridges over the two branches of Elk River, requiring considerably more work than anticipated. Requests court appoint "two discreet persons to view the said bridges and make report ... of the value of building the said bridges." Court declines and directs that Thomas be paid 7,000 lbs/tbco as previously agreed.

Petition of Herman Kinkey. Postponed.

f.41 (DSC02189)

==

Petition of Daniel Hukill. States that he served as constable for Bohemia Hundred in 1720 and was required to collect from a list of taxables. Edmund Butcher reported only himself as a taxable for his household, but Hukill afterwards spoke with one John Walker who said he also lived at Butcher's house and should be listed there. Butcher refused to acknowledge responsibility, and Hukill ended up paying Walker's tax. Hukill asks court to credit him in current year for what he had paid to cover Walker. Court allows Hukill 113½ lbs/tbco in current levy.

Court adjourned and reconvened morning of 17 November.

Petition of Herman Kinkey. States that he lives by Elk River ferry and keeps a public house there. Asks that he be made ferry keeper. Court approves and allows Kinkey 3,000 lbs/tbco for keeping the ferry from this day until next November court.

Memorandum concerning ferrymen.* Justices agree that if any valid complaint is made against ferrymen in the county to two justices of the peace, they are empowered to relieve the incumbent and appoint another in his stead.

f.42 (DSC02190)

==

Petition of John Jawart, Benjanin Pearce, James Alexander and John Smith. States that they were appointed by Charles Calvert, governor of Maryland, to conduct a survey of New Munster, which they did over four days in the summer. They ask to be compensated for their effort. Court awards them 250 lbs/tbco each from present levy.

Petition of Adam Wallace. Submits an account of his expenses totaling £6/11/0, mainly doctor's fees, for the care and cure of Elizabeth Jones, "a distressed and distempered woman." (See her petition on f.35.) Court allows him 1,572 lbs/tbco.

Petition of Barnard Brock.* States that he has faithfully paid his taxes as a citizen of Cecil County but recently broke his arm. It is in a deplorable condition and has little chance of being fixed because of his age and feebleness. Asks that he be removed as a taxable from the constable's list. An attestation in support of Brock is presented to court, signed by Evan James, Stephen Ross, Isaac James, Thomas Cochran and Hugh Ross. Court approves and allows him 200 lbs/tbco.

f.43 (DSC02190)

===

Petition of Richard Warner and William Briggs. Petitioners state that they arrived in the province after the time at which the constables collected their lists of taxables. Notwithstanding, the constable included them in his list along with four who accompanied them—Warner's three servants and Briggs's slave. Ask the court to credit them in this year's levy for the tobacco they previously paid. Granted.

Petition of Gunning Bradford.* States that in previous November court he had delivered an account amounting to £14/2/2 for expenses in keeping the governor and counsel at his house. Court approved at the time, and he was "entered on the file" but later removed for some reason. Asks that he be given credit again. Court approves.

Court adjourned until March session.

f.44 (DSC02191)

===

March Court 1722
Court convened 2nd Tuesday, 12 March 1722, at Elk River, continued to 16 March.* Following commissioners present: Mr. Matt. Van Bebber, Col. Benjamin Pearce, Mr. Samuel Alexander, Mr. Edward Jackson, Mr. Stephen Hollingsworth, Mr. James Alexander. Also present John Hack, sheriff, and Stephen Knight, clerk. Francis Mauldin, one of the justices of the commission for Oyer and Terminer of 3 November 1722, takes oaths and takes seat on bench. Henry Ward also sits. Court adjourned .

Court adjourned and reconvened 13 March. Mr. John Jawert joins court. William Rumsey is sworn in as deputy clerk and takes usual oaths and

Oath of Abjuration and the Test. No petitions preferred this day. Court adjourned .

Court adjourned and reconvened 14 March.

Petition of Nathaniel Sapington and Thomas Severson. States that the King's road runs between their plantations and causes many problems. Ask to turn it in a way that will cause no inconvenience to the public. Court approves, to be done at petitioners' charge.

f.45 (DSC02191)
==
Petition of Thomas Hynson. States that a public road runs through his plantation which is inconvenient for county service and detrimental to himself. Asks that he may turn it. Court approves, petitioner to cover costs.

Petition of Joseph Wood.* States that a road was laid out by order of the court from head of Back Creek to the road going to New Castle but was never properly cleared and is dangerous to travelers. Asks court to appoint men to oversee the clearing of said road. Court directs that a clause be inserted in the overseer's warrant for that hundred to "clear the said road as far toward New Castle as where the Pennsilvanians leave off." Joseph Wood appointed inspector.

f.46 (DSC20192)
==
Court adjourned and reconvened 2 April (continuation of March Court). Commissioners present: Mr. Matt. Van Bebber, Col. Benjamin Pearce, Mr. John Jawert, Mr. Edward Jackson, Mr. Francis Mauldin, Mr. Samuel Alexander, Mr. Stephen Hollingsworth, Mr. James Alexander. Also present; John Hack, sheriff; Stephen Knight, clerk.

Petition of Matthew Matthiason. States that he lives at James Town on Sassafras River where a ferry and several public houses had formerly been located but were no longer there. People still come there looking for a ferry. Matthiason asks to be allowed to sell drink to them. Court permits him to keep an ordinary or public house.

f.47 (DSC20192)

===

Petition of John Ryland. Asks to be discharged from being ranger of Cecil, being willing to give up his commission. Rejected.

Court adjourned and reconvened several days without any business recorded. Following commissioners present: Mr. John Jawert, Mr. James Alexander, Col. Benjamin Pearce, Mr. Stephen Hollingsworth, Mr. Edward Jackson.

Court adjourned and reconvened on Saturday, 6 April.

Petition of Joseph Burchmore.* Complains that he is unjustly detained as a servant to John Kimber under a claimed indenture agreement which Burchmore says was "surreptitiously obtained." Asks Court for relief. Court orders Kimber to give petitioner "his freedom dues according to law" and 400 lbs/tbco for the time of his over-servitude.

Court adjourned until June session.

f.48 (DSC02193)

===

June Court 1723

Court convened 2nd Tuesday, 11 June, at Elk River, continued to 15 June.
Following commissioners present: Mr. John Jawert, Mr. Henry Ward, Mr. Francis Mauldin, Mr. Stephen Hollingsworth, Col. Benjamin Pearce, Mr. Samuel Alexander, Mr. Edward Jackson, Mr. James Alexander. Also present, John Hack, sheriff, and Stephen Knight, clerk.

Petition of the upper inhabitants of Cecil County.* States that there is no road from the ford at Head of Elk to New Castle or to Christiana Bridge because the road ordered by the Court had not been laid out, so travelers are forced to use the New Munster road, while others go to French Town instead of Head of Elk. They note that the Welsh community in New Castle County had cleared and marked a road through their area as far as it extends. Asks court to order construction of a road from Head of Elk to connect with the said road and also a road to Christiana Bridge. Signed by William Bristow, Gunning Bedford, John Buchanan, Thomas Russell, Adam

Wallace, Bartile Johnson, Stephen Onion, James Wallace, Peter Barker, John Hack, Martin Alexander, William Thomas, Simon Johnson, Francis Alexander, Henry Runalls, _____ Hendrickson, Richard Dobson, Thomas Jacobs. Court grants petition and appoints William Bristow as overseer of Bohemia Hundred and Thomas Jacobs to see that roads are laid out.

f.49 (DSC02193)
==

Petiton of John Hinkley. Postponed.

Summons ordered for Peter Cormack to appear in Court next day.

Court adjourned and reconvened on Wednesday, 12 June. Mr. Abell Van Burkelo asks court to enter into the record that he is declining to be an attorney of the court. Granted.

Court adjourned and reconvened on Thursday, 13 June.

Petition of inhabitants of Milford Hundred.* States that a road is needed from New Munster road at David Alexander's to the Church road near Stephen Hollingsworth's mill. Asks court to order such a road be laid out. Signed by Alexander White, Martin Cartmill, Thomas Brown, John Segar, Jonathan Curtis, Joseph Teell, Tobias James, Joseph Hollingsworth, Thomas Sharp, George Robinson, Richard Cleyton, James Andrews, Robert Holey, John Finlow, James Young, Phillip Davis, James Mafet. Court grants petition and appoints Jonathan Curtis and Martin Cartmell as inspectors to see that road is laid out and cleared.

f.50 (DSC02194)
==

Petition of John Hinkley. Asks that summons be issued for James Jackson, Jun., and Joseph Slider to appear as witness for him in case against Peter Carmacke. Summons ordered.

Petition of Rees Hinton. Rejected.**Petition of Stephen Onion. Postponed.** Court orders a warrant be issued for Mary Seale to appear in Court to answer to Stephen Onion. Warrant given to Nathaniel Worley, deputed constable, to deliver.

31

Court adjourned and reconvened on Saturday, 15 June. Mary Seale appears per summons.

Petition of Stephen Onion.* States that partners in England sent indentured servants to him, viz. Matthias Seale, his wife Mary and children, Matthias, Joseph, Samuel, James and Mary. Seale had died 9 months after his arrival and now Onion states that Mary Seale claims she has no obligation under the agreement and refuses to obey his orders. Asks court to order Mary Seale and her children to serve Onion "either by the indenture or by the customs of the country." Court judges that Mary Seale and her children cannot be held as servants under the indenture. Orders Onion to take care and charge of the five children and bring them into August Court.

f.51 (DSC02194)
==
Petition of Elizabeth Pope. Continued until next court.

Petition of John Hinkley.* Complains that he had served Peter Carmicke faithfully for a full term of four years but Carmicke refuses to discharge him or pay him his freedom dues as required in the province. Carmicke appears and claims that Hinkley did not work for him on 12 April last. Hinkley makes oath that he did work that day and produces John Slider and Joanes Umbers as witness on his behalf. Court considers the case and orders Carmicke to give Hinkley his freedom dues according to Act of Assembly.

Court adjourned until August session.

f.52 (DSC02195)
==

August Court 1723
Court convened 2nd Tuesday, 13 August 1723, at Elk River, continued to 17 August. Following commissioners present: Mr. Francis Mauldin, Mr. Stephen Hollingsworth, Col. Benjamin Pearce, Mr. James Alexander, Mr. Edward Jackson, Mr. Samuel Alexander. Also present, John Hack, sheriff, and Stephen Knight, clerk. Read the Commission of Peace dated 5 Aug

1723. Justices mentioned therein take the usual oaths. Court adjourned till next day.

Court adjourned and reconvened Wednesday, 14 August. Following commissioners present: Mr. John Jawert, Mr. Edward Jackson, Mr. Francis Mauldin, Mr. Samuel Alexander, Col. Benjamin Pearce, Mr. Stephen Hollingsworth, Mr. John Baldwin, Mr. James Alexander.

Petition of Milford Hundred inhabitants.* States that although a road had been laid out from "the branches of Elk River to the Church at Northeast" but it is "difficult, dangerous and troublesome to maintain by reason of crossing several branches particularly the east branch of Northeast River twice." Also, the original road was only a bridle road, but a cart road is needed. They ask that a new road may be laid out. Signed by Francis Wallace, Abraham Hollingsworth, Joseph Hollingsworth, John Spie, Alexander White, James MacClear, Walt Carr, Reneer VanCoolen, William Maffitt, Samuel Maffitt, Samuel Bond, Tobias James, Matthew Hodgson, Hugh Lawson, Jonathan Curtis, William Gorrell, Thomas Sharpe, John Thomas, John Mare, Zebulon Hollingsworth, Robert Holy, Martin Cartmill. Court grants petition; appoints Stephen Hollingsworth as inspector to see that road is laid out without problem to any of the inhabitants.

f.53 (DSC02195)
==
Petition of Edward Jackson. Asks that court order a road to be cleared from the ironworks to his house. Court so orders.

Petition of Henry Ward. Postponed.

Petition of Edward Jackson and James Campbell. States that a road had never been cleared from Susquehanna Lower Ferry to Octoraro but one is needed. Asks court to order one be done. Court so directs; appoints James Campbell as inspector.

f.54 (DSC02196)
==
Petition of Mary Enerster. Rejected.

Court adjourned and reconvened Thursday, 15 August.

Petition of Henry Ward. Rejected.

Court adjourned and reconvened Friday, 16 August.

Petition of John Jones. States that he has a case depending in which he is accused by Sheriff John Hack but that his attorney is David McBride is now absent. He fears judgment will be found against him for lack of an attorney as had been the case previously and asks court to appoint one for him. Court agrees and appoints John Johnson as attorney for Jones.

Court adjourned and reconvened Saturday, 17 August.

f.55 (DSC92196)
===
Petition of Richard Touchstone. Touchstone keeps the upper ferry on the Susquehanna and complains that it is a hardship to pay for a license while not having a road cleared to the ferry. Asks that a road be cleared from Nottingham to the ferry. Court grants petition; directs Touchstone to clear a road without causing problems for the inhabitants.

Court adjourned until November session.

November Court 1723
Court convened 12 November at Elk River, continued to 19 November. Following commissioners present: Mr. John Jawert, Mr. Francis Mauldin, Col. Benjamin Pearce, Mr. Edward Jackson, Mr. John Baldwin, Mr. James Alexander, Mr. Richard Thompson, Mr. Henry Ward, Mr. Stephen Hollingsworth. Also present, John Hack, sheriff, and Stephen Knight, clerk.

Petition of Peter Bouchelle. States that he has for some time kept and cared for John Browne who is ill and incapable of providing for himself. Asks that he be made levy free or that court provide some assistance. Court allows 300 lbs/tbco to Bouchelle for care of Browne.

f.56 (DSC02197)

===

Petition of Robert Holy. Rejected.

Petition of John Hack. Asks for an addition to his allowance for keeping Bohemia Ferry. Rejected.

Petition of Richard Rutter. States that in March 1721 court had "put to him for a certain Jane Rudd's child unto Susana Granger" but that no allowance had been provided to Granger. Asks that allowance be provided to Granger for her keeping the child. Court allows her 1,500 lbs/tbco "for nursing and keeping the base born child of Jane Rudd."

Court adjourned and reconvened on 13 November.

Petition of Herman Kinkey. Postponed.

Petition of John Hack. Asks for allowance "due him for the election of the delegates of the county." Court directs he be given allowance "according to the law this levy." Amount not specified.

Petition of John Hinckley and John Bishop. Concerning Unice Bishop. Rejected.

Petition of Joanna Tayner. Rejected.

f.57 (DSC02197)

===

Petition of Samuel Brice et al. States that they had attended court as evidences for the lord proprietor in case against Isaac Taylor and Elisha Gatchel during June and August Court sessions. Asks that they be paid for their time; Samuel Brice for 10 days, James Almond for five days and Daniel Smith for seven days. Court approves.

Court adjourned and reconvened Thursday, 14 November.

Petition of Henry Hendrickson and James Panton. Hendrickson states that he had made a mistake in his list of taxables as constable in 1722 and charged Panton with five taxables rather than four as he should have. Panton was consequently charged 130½ lbs/tbco more in "the staff's books" than he should have been. Ask that Panton be given credit in current levy for same amount accordingly. Granted.

Petition of William Mainard. Rejected.

Petition of Col. Ephraim Aug. Herman. Postponed.

Petition of James Proud. Asks for an attorney be assigned him in an action against Matthias Van Bebber. Court assigns Joshua George to represent Proud.

f.58 (DSC02198)

==

Petition of William Garish. States that he has been provided an allowance as an object of charity for some years and asks that it be continued for the next year. Court allows him 1,200 lbs/tbco from current levy.

Petition of Charles Thomas. Complains that he had been charged for three taxables by Sheriff John Hack in the levy but should have been charged only one. Asks for relief in current levy. Court allows him 282 lbs/tbco credit in current levy.

Petition of Joanna Dampeir.* States that she is a poor widow with children and has spent what little her husband left her. She is very lame and cannot live without assistance. She has been advised to see a doctor but cannot afford it. Requests court grant her 2,000 lbs/tbco. Court allows her 1,200 lbs/tbco.

f.59 (DSC02198)

==

Petition of Sarah Prue. States that she is feeble and impotent and has been an object of charity for three years. Asks court to continue her allowance. Court allows her 1,500 lbs/tbco.

Petition of Edward Lang. States that he attended court as evidence for the lord proprietor against Isaac Taylor and Elisha Gatchell. Asks that he be granted allowance as provided in law. Court allows him 30 lbs/tbco per day of attendance.

Court adjourned and reconvened on Friday, 5 November.

Petition of Herman Kinkey. Postponed.

f.60 (DSC02199)

==

Petition of Barnard Brock. States that he has lived in the county for many years but is now impotent and unable to support himself. Asks for assistance. Court allows him 150 lbs/tbco from current levy.

Court adjourned and reconvened Tuesday, 19 November. Proceeds "to finish laying the Levy."

Court adjourned until March Court.

March Court 1723

Court convened 10 March 1723, at Elk River, continued to 14 March. Following Commissioners present: Mr. John Jawert, Mr. Richard Thompson, Mr. Francis Mauldin, Mr. James Alexander, Mr. Edward Jackson, Mr. Stephen Hollingsworth. Also present, John Hack, Sheriff and Stephen Knight, Clerk.

Read the petition of John Astle.

f.61-62 (DSC02199, DSC02200) No entries

f.63 (DSC02200)

==

June Court 1724

Court convened 9 June 1724, at Elk River, continued to 11 June. Following commissioners present: Mr. John Jawert, Col. Benjamin Pearce, Mr. Francis Mauldin, Mr. Edward Jackson, Mr. James Alexander, Mr. Richard Thompson, Mr. Henry Ward. Also present, John Hack, sheriff, and Stephen Knight, clerk.

Petition of Sheriff John Hack.* States that he has a certain Robert Dutch in his custody who has been sentenced to be hanged on 19 June. He is concerned with the insufficiency of the gaol [jail] and asks for "sufficient standing guard to secure the prisoner till he is brought to condign punishment." Also asks that the constables of the several hundreds be summoned to report to his jail at 8:00 on 19 June to assist him in bringing the prisoner to the place of execution. Court directs that the sheriff summon two men "to watch and ward" the prisoner who will be paid for their service. Court also directs that the constables be summoned as requested.

Court adjourned until August session.

f.64 (DSC20201)

==

August Court 1724

Court convened 11 August 1724, at Elk River, continued to 15 August. Following commissioners present: Mr. John Jawert, Mr. James Alexander, Maj. Francis Mauldin, Mr. John Baldwin, Capt. Richard Thompson, Mr. Stephen Hollingsworth, Capt. Edward Jackson. Also present, John Hack, sheriff, and Stephen Knight, clerk.

Petition of Daniel Davis. States that he lives on main road near the ironworks and is frequently pressed by travelers for services. Asks for a license to keep a public house. Granted.

Petition of Matthias Van Bebber.* Complains about his servant Garrett Bann who refuses to obey him. States that Bann had arrived without an indenture and should be subject to the Act of Assembly for such cases.

Court directs Daniel Hukill to bring Bann into Court to answer the complaint. After Bann appears the court judges that he be obliged to serve Van Bebber "for five years commencing from the time of the ship's anchoring in Maryland that brought the said Garrett Bann in, which arrival was the 25th November 1722. Also the Court orders that the Sheriff take the said Garret Bann to the whipping post and give him 25 lashes upon the bare back well laid on."

f.65 (DSC20201)
===
Petition of James Heath. States that he was granted a tract called Heath's Outlet on the north side of the Sassafras River containing 1,000 acres, 100 of which were sold. A white oak stood at a corner of the property and on the northeast line of another tract called Painters Rest and was the first corner point of Pullens Refuge. There is some confusion about the location of the tree and Heath asks that a commission be formed to investigate. Court appoints Col. Benjamin Pearce, Maj. John Dowdall, John Baldwin and Col. John Ward as commissioners.

f.66 (DSC02202)
===
Petition if Ephraim Augustine Herman and John Campbell. Ask court to permit them to build a new main road at their own expense from the (Bohemia) Manor gate to the road that leads to the courthouse. Granted.

Petition of John Dowdall. States that he owns a tract called None Such in Finland for which some of the corner marking trees are decayed. Asks for a commission to investigate and confirm the boundaries. Court appoints Col. John Ward, Col. Benjamin Pearce, Nicholas Ridgley and George Veazey as commissioners.

Court adjourned until next session.

f.67 (DSC02202)
===

November Court 1724
Court convened 19 November at Elk River, continued to 14 November. Following commissioners present: Mr. John Jawert, Mr. Stephen Hol-

lingsworth, Col. B. Pearce, Maj. Mauldin, Capt. Richard Thompson, Capt. Edward Jackson, Mr. John Baldwin, Mr. Henry Ward, Mr. James Alexander. Also present, John Hack sheriff, and Stephen Knight, clerk.

Petition of Peter Bayard. States that he has an old negro slave name Dick who is unable to work and that he maintains him for charity and has continued to pay taxes for him on the annual levy. Asks that the court make him levy free for the future. Court excuses Bayard from listing negro Dick as a taxable.

f.68 (DSC02203)
==
Petition of Lewis England. States that his home is on the King's highway between Susquehanna Lower Ferry and Northeast and that he has been asked by travelers for lodging and refreshment both for themselves and their animals, which has been a considerable inconvenience for him. Asks that he be granted a license to keep an ordinary. Granted.

Petition of Thomas Johnson.* States that the county does not at present have a ranger and he would like to be appointed to same by the governor which requires their recommendation. Asks that they provide a letter recommending him and vouching for his character. Court agrees and provides him with a recommendation.

f.69 (DSC02203)
==
Petition of John Hack. States that the past November the court had approved him to be keeper of Bohemia Ferry with an allowance of 5,000 lbs/tbco, but the clerk had not provided notice of this to the committee for laying the levy and he had not been paid. Asks that court now provide him his payment and renew his agreement for keeping Bohemia Ferry for another year at the same allowance. Granted.

Petition of Johanna Dempper (Demppah). States that she is lame and unable to help herself or live without assistance. Asks court to provide her an allowance of 1,200 lbs/tbco. Court directs that she be considered a poor pensioner and given the requested allowance.

40

f.70 (DSC02204)

==

Petition of the vestry of North Elk Parish Richard Dobson, register. States that they cannot finish the new church addition without assistance from the county. Requests that the court assess 5 lbs/tbco for each taxable in the parish. Granted.

Petition of Sarah Prue. States that she is not able to care for herself and has been supported by the county in the past with an allowance of 1,500 lbs/tbco. Asks that the same be continued for the next year. Court allows her 1,000 lbs/tbco from current levy.

f.71 (DSC02204)

==

Petition of Col. James Maxwell of Baltimore County. States that he is owner of a 480-acre tract called Newhall whose boundary maker trees are much decayed and that the people who can prove the location of said bounders are now very old and infirm. Asks that a commission be formed to investigate and confirm the bounds. Court appoints Capt. Edward Jackson, Capt. Richard Thompson, Capt. Alexander and Mr. John Smith as commissioners.

Petition of John Chick. States that he lives near the eastern bound of Bohemia Manor and has been designated as a taxable for both North Sassafras Hundred and Bohemia Manor Hundred for three years and has thereby paid 297 lbs/tbco more than he should have. Asks that he be given credit for same in current levy. Granted.

f.72 (DSC02205)

==

Petition of James Andrews et al.* Petitioners state that they have lately built a mill on a branch of the Elk River but there are no roads leading to it. Asks that court direct roads be built from the mill to the King's highway leading to Elk landing and to the highway leading to North East. If so, they will make the highways at their charge and not intrude on anyone's enclosures. Signed by James Andrews, James Hobetts, Rodger Lawson, James Mathel, John Hogsitt, Abram Hollingsworth, Morgan Patten, Thomas Sharp, Robert Holy. Court approves; to be done at their charge.

Petition of Gavin Hutchison. States that the court had directed him to bring his servant Jean Morrispowell to court at the completion of her term of service for judgment considering damages to Hutchison because Morrispowell had been delivered of a base-born child while in his service. Hutchison has accordingly brought Morrispowell to court and asks for their decision on the matter. Court judges that Morrispowell should serve Hutchison an additional half-year "for the trouble of his house."

f.73 (DSC02205)

===

Petition of Susannah Granger. States that the court had assigned her to nurse the child of Jane Reed (Rudd), the servant of Ralph Rutter, and she had done so from 9 November 1723 to 17 June 1724. Asks Court for payment accordingly. Court allows Granger 700 lbs/tbco.

Petition of Benjamin Allen.* States that he had submitted a note to them through Capt. Edward Jackson for bounty on one wolf head and 38 squirrel heads and now requests payment for same. Court orders he be paid (no amount stated.)

Petition of Cornelius McCormack.* States that the past November he had submitted a note for bounty on 86 squirrels heads and five crows but that "by some mistake" he had been underpaid by 256 lbs/tbco. Asks that he be given credit in the levy for same. Court allows him credit for 100 lbs/tbco from present levy.

f.74 (DSC02206)

===

Petitions of Charles Carroll, endorsed by John Smith. Carroll had requested Smith to ask Court on his behalf to form a commission to investigate the boundaries of four tracts which Carroll had acquired from William FitzRedmond: Durrow (300 acres), Doe Hill (50 acres), KillaVilly (200 acres) and Derryheel (1,900 acres); dated 21 July 1724. Smith accordingly requests court to appoint a commission. Court appoints Capt. Edward Jackson, Mr. John Baldwin, Capt. James Alexander and Capt. Richard Thompson as commissioners.

Petition of Herman Kinkey. States that he has kept the ferry at Elk River for the past year with no complaints. Asks that he be allowed to continue the same for another year at the same rate. Granted.

f.75 (DSC02206)
===

Petition of Ephraim Aug. Herman. States that he owns two tracts, Bohemia Manor and Middle Neck, which had belonged to his ancestors and whose boundaries are much decayed, especially at the eastern end, causing several disputes. Asks court to form a committee to investigate. Court appoints Col. Benjamin Pearce, Col. John Ward, John Baldwin and William Rumsey.

Petition of Jane Davis.* States that her husband Francis Davis was indebted to Hugh Matthews for 30 shillings and that in her husband's absence Matthews obtained an attachment by which he seized from her items of much greater value. She afterwards took wheat to him to pay the debt and reclaim her goods, but he refuses to release them. Asks court to order return her goods. Court so orders.

f.76 (DSC02207)
===

Petition of Thomas Pimm.* States that he, an inhabitant of the county for 12 years and now 73 years of age, is afflicted with sickness and lameness and unable to support himself. Asks court to provide him an allowance. Court allows him 400 lbs/tbco from present levy.

Court adjourned until next session.

f.77 (DSC02207)
===

March Court 1724
Court convened 13 March 1724, at Elk River. Following commissioners present: Mr. John Jawert, Mr. James Alexander, Maj. Francis Mauldin, Capt. Edward Jackson, Capt. Richard Thompson, Mr. Stephen Hollingsworth, Mr. John Baldwin, Col. B. Pearce, Mr. Henry Ward. Also present, John Smith, sheriff, and Stephen Knight, clerk.

Petition of John Hamond and inhabitants of north side of Octoraro Creek. Ask court to order a road from north side of Octoraro to the Conestoga Road. Signed by Abraham Colleck, George Emmey. Court approves, with the inhabitants to clear the road at their charge; John Hamond appointed overseer.

Petition of Cornelius McCormack et al.* States that the petitioners had laid out a road for sundry inhabitants of Susquehanna Hundred to roll tobacco to Susquehanna River and kept it clear at their own charge, but now the road is likely to be stopped up by others. Asks that the court order that the road be allowed to stay as is. Signed by Cornelius MacCormack, William Curer, Samuel Buie, George Martain, Richard Abiall, John Partall, John Longue. Court directs that road remain as it was cleared.

f.78 (DSC02208)
===
Petition of John Alexander. States that he has been asked by sundry citizens of the county to practice as an attorney so he now requests that the court admit him as an attorney to the court. Court approves, he taking the usual oaths and subscribing to the Oath of Abjuration and Test.

Petition of James Heath. States that he has a tract called Heaths Outlet containing 1,000 acres surveyed for him on the north side of the Sassafras River in 1701, out of which he had conveyed a 100-acre parcel. He asks court to form a commission to investigate the bounds. Court appoints Col. Pearce, Col. Ward, Maj. Dowdall and Mr. John Baldwin. (This is very similar to Heath's petition in August court, f.65; no explanation as to why it is being repeated. See also June court 1727, f.111.)

f.79 (DSC02208)
===
Petition of Richard Whitton. States that some eight years before the court had bound a child named Benjamin Cox, son of Giddion Cox, deceased, to him as an apprentice and servant until age 21, and Whitton agreed to teach him to read and write and the trade of a cooper. Whitton says that the youth has taken to running away and is still away so Whitton asks to be released from his obligations and that the youth be assigned to his uncle, Benjamin Cox, or someone else. Court judges that Whitton be

released of his covenants and that Benjamin Cox, Jun., be bound as apprentice to his uncle Benjamin Cox, until of age, at which time he will be given a horse, a new suit, new hat, two shirts, a pair of shoes and stockings.

Petition of several Alexanders, dated 10 March 1724. States that a previous order of the court provided for a road from Hollingsworth Mill towards New Castle but that the path of the road is disadvantageous because it leads through a swampy area and over hills. Ask that court approve a different path a little above the present one; work to be done by the inhabitants. Signed by James Alexander, David Alexander, Moses Alexander, James Alexander, Arthur Alexander and Elias Alexander. Court approves and appoints James Alexander and Stephen Hollingsworth as inspectors.

f.80 (DSC02209)
===

Petition of Col. Benjamin Pearce. States that he owns a 1,000-acre tract called The Rounds on the south side of Little Bohemia River and that a certain Thomas Pearce is making claims regarding the boundaries but has not brought an ejectment proceeding to make his case. Asks court to form a commission to investigate the bounds so they can be confirmed and recorded. Court appoints Col. Herman, Major Dowdall, John Baldwin and Nicholas Ridgley as commissioners.

Court adjourned until first Monday in May.

f.81 (DSC02209)
===

Court convened 3 May 1725. Following commissioners present: Mr. John Jawert, Maj. Francis Mauldin, Col. Benjamin Pearce, Capt. James Alexander, Capt. Edward Jackson, Capt. Richard Thompson, Mr. Henry Ward, Mr. John Baldwin. Also present, John Smith, sheriff, and Stephen Knight, clerk.

Petition of Mary Parsons, administratrix of William Parsons, deceased.*
States that she has two slaves aged 80 years and over 70 years and "unable to earn their victuals." Asks court to declare them levy free. Court

rules that one of them, named Tom, is made levy free. [No mention of the other.]

Petition of Phillip Loyd and Matthias Van Bebber. Petitioners state that they own a tract of land called Saint Augustine's Manor which lies "partly in the county" at the eastern bounds of Bohemia Manor and that the boundaries are in dispute. Asks the court to form a commission to investigate and take depositions from knowledgeable persons who are aged and infirm. Court appoints Col. Benjamin Pearce, John Baldwin, William Rumsey and John Copson as commissioners.

f.82 (DSC02210)
==
Petition of James Heath. States that he owns a tract called Heath's Range, except for a 200-acre parcel which had been sold, and is concerned about the bounds at the head and branches of Sassafras Creek and on branches of Appoquinomy Creek. Asks court to appoint a commission to investigate and confirm the bounds. Court appoints Col. Benjamin Pearce, Col. John Ward, John Baldwin and Capt. Richard Thompson as commissioners.

Court is adjourned until June session.

June Court 1725
Court convened 8 1725, June at Elk River, continued until 11 June. Following commissioners present: Mr. John Jawert, Capt. Richard Thompson, Maj. Francis Mauldin, Mr. Henry Ward, Col. Benjamin Pearce, Capt. Edward Jackson, Capt. James Alexander, Mr. Stephen Hollingsworth, Mr. John Baldwin. Also present, John Smith, sheriff, and Stephen Knight, clerk.

f.83 (DSC02210)
==
Petition of Joseph Young.* States that he has cared for a Benjamin Clark for some years and paid for him as a taxable in the levy though he is "unable to earn even his own victuals" because of an incurable malady that frequently throws him into seizures and fits, as is well known in the neighborhood. Asks court to make him levy free. Granted.

Petition of William Johnson. States that he is under a recognizance bond of £50 sterling to "persecute the body of William Humphreys into an act of felony" but the date of the trial at next assizes is a long time off. In the meantime Johnson does not have the use of his clothes "which was found in the custody of the said Humphreys" which is a great inconvenience. Asks that the court order that the clothes be turned over to him. Court rejects petition.

Court adjourned until August session.

f.84 (DSC02211)
===

August Court 1725

Court convened 10 August at Elk River, continued until 13 August. Following commissioners present: Mr. John Jawert, Mr. Stephen Hollingsworth, Maj. Francis Mauldin, Capt. Richard Thompson, Capt. Edward Jackson, Col. Benjamin Pearce, Capt. James Alexander, Mr. John Baldwin. Also present, John Smith, sheriff, and Stephen Knight, clerk.

Petition of Edward Smith of Baltimore County.* States that about six years previous a William Burney had arrived from Ireland with a large family of small children and settled next to him in Baltimore but that in a short time they were affected with a long sickness and with no means to survive, at which point Smith took them into his own house and took care for them as best he could. Five died and the others recovered. Smith paid for the burials. William Burney himself died but before dying asked that Smith take care of his one son named Thomas, then about six years old, until he comes of age, which Smith has endeavored to do as though his own son. Last June the said Thomas was suddenly missing without explanation, to the surprise of Smith and his neighbors. Smith made great effort to locate the boy and has found that he was secretly taken in the night and out of Baltimore by one Thomas Reynolds of Cecil County. Smith states that he understands that "the act aforesaid committed by the said Reynolds is by the Common Law indictable and highly punishable" but that it must be tried in the county where it was committed. Smith asks Court to have Reynolds and the boy brought into court and make such order as they deem appropriate according to law and justice. The Court issues a summons and Reynolds is brought into court. Court orders that Reynolds deliver Thomas Burney to Smith and orders Smith to post recognizance bond of £20 for Thomas Burney's appearance in November court in Baltimore County.

f.85 (DSC02211)

===

Petition of George Douglas. States that he entered into an indenture agreement with two servants, William Keeting and Thomas Farrell, for a four-year period but that they had departed before the expiration of their terms. Asks court to have them brought in and answer to him. Court issues summons and Keeting and Farrel are brought in. After hearing the case, court orders Keeting to serve Douglas eight more days and Farrell to serve Douglas four more days.

f.86 DSC02212

===

Petition of Ephraim Aug. Herman. States that he owns a large tract called Great Bohemia Manor whose boundaries are disputed by Philemon Loyd, Esq. and Matthias Van Bebber. The matter had been previously investigated by a commission, but Herman states that new witnesses are now available who can provide additional relevant information which might change the findings. Asks that court form a commission to investigate. Court appoints Col. Benjamin Pearce, John Baldwin, William Rumsey and John Veazey as commissioners.

Court adjourned until November session.

November Court 1725

Court convened 9 November 1725, at Elk River, continued until 13 November. Following commissioners present: Mr. John Jawert, Mr. Stephen Hollingsworth, Maj. Francis Mauldin, Capt. Richard Thompson, Capt. Edward Jackson, Col. Benjamin Pearce, Capt. James Alexander, Mr. John Baldwin, Mr. Henry Ward. Also present, John Smith, sheriff, and Stephen Knight, clerk.

f.87 DSC02212

==

Petition of James Veysey (Veazey). States that he lives by the Elk Ferry and that two different roads lead from the ferry, one to North East and one to the main road. He complains that this is a problem for him and that only one road is necessary and asks that court allow him to close one of the roads. Court sends Edward Jackson and Stephen Hollingsworth to investigate, and they report back that the road by Veazey's house is useless. Court orders that it be closed.

Petition of Robert Penington. States that the present road from Point of Bohemia Ferry where John Ryland, Jun., now lives to Mr. Sutton's mill is injurious to him and that another road could be laid which would be better and more commodious to travelers. Asks court for approval to turn the road accordingly, at his own charge. Court grants petition and appoints John Baldwin as inspector to ensure the road is well cleared.

Petition of Edward Jackson. Complains that the road from Octoraro to Lower Susquehanna Ferry is a problem for him and asks for court to appoint two magistrates to investigate and make recommendation on the matter. Court appoints Francis Mauldin and Stephen Hollingsworth to see a convenient road laid out.

f.88 (DSC02213)

==

Petition of John Paine.* States that he is "very ancient and past his labor and it has pleased God of late to take his eyesight from him so that he cannot see to walk." Asks court to make him levy free. Court directs that he be allowed 200 lbs/tbco as a poor pensioner.

Petition of Thomas Pimm, a poor pensioner. Asks for support from the county. Court allows him 200 lbs/tbco.

Petition of Sarah Prue, a poor pensioner. Asks for support from the county. Court allows her 1,000 lbs/tbco, "as usual."

49

Petition of Joanna Dampier. States that she has not been able to support herself for several years and was awarded 1,200 lb/tbco by the court last year, "but your petitioner having no friend at Court to get her allowance entered in the Levy List last year she was deprived of the same." Court orders that she be allowed 2,700 lbs/tbco in present levy. (See November court 1723, f.58.)

Petition of Rodger Lawson, Joseph Steel et al. States that they are residents of a tract called Society which is "depending on only one single bound" that might be lost or destroyed. Ask Court to form a commission to confirm the boundaries. Signed by Roger Lawson, Joseph Steel, Robert Holy, James Andrews, Thomas Sharp, John Sougar (Seegar). Court appoints Capt. Edward Jackson, Capt. Richard Thompson, Stephen Hollingsworth and John Smith, as commissioners.

f.89 (DSC02213)
==
Petition of Benjamin Cox. States that he owns two tracts called Peter's Field and Clements Hills on north side of Sassafras River and that their western boundary is being disputed. Asks court to appoint a commission to investigate and confirm the boundaries. Court appoints Mr. Ridgley, John Baldwin, William Rumsey and John Veazey as commissioners.

Petition of Ephraim Aug. Herman. States that the road from Choptank to Delaware between the plantations of John OCahan and Joseph Woods on Back Creek, and bordering his own property, Bohemia Manor, is old and neglected and needs to be cleared. Asks that court order that it be cleared and pledges to do so at his charge. Court approves and appoints John Baldwin and William Rumsey as inspectors.

Court adjourned until March Session.

f.90 (DSC02214)
==

March Court 1725
Court convened 8 March 1725 at Elk River, continued until 10 March, then adjourned until 2 May. Following Commissioners present: Mr. Francis Mauldin, Mr. Stephen Hollingsworth, Col. Benjamin Pearce, Mr. Henry

Ward, Capt. Edward Jackson, Mr. John Baldwin, Capt. James Alexander, Capt. Richard Thompson. Also present, John Smith, sheriff, and Stephen Knight, clerk.

Petition of Angell Davis, widow. States that her plantation is now short of rail timber and she cannot keep the lane through her property in good repair. Asks that she be allowed to turn the road to go by the outside of her property. Court approves, subject to review and possible alteration by Col. Benjamin Pearce and John Baldwin.

Court adjourned until 2 May

f.91 (DSC02214)
==
Petition of James Christie, et al, prisoners of the sheriff. States that that they are poor distressed prisoners held by the sheriff because of their debts but are qualified for release under the Act of the Assembly for Relief and Release of Poor Distressed Prisoners. They are "ready to yield up all and sundry our effects upon oath for the use of our creditors" and wish to be qualified as the law directs in order to obtain their certificates before next court, time being very short. Signed by James Christie, William Burton, William Mainard and Thomas Brown. Court grants petition, "they qualifying themselves according to Act for Relief of Poor Debtors."

Petition of Henry Ward. States that he owns a tract called Poplar Neck at south side of the mouth of Elk River, the first bounder tree of which is blown over. Asks court to form a commission to examine and confirm the bounds. Court appoints Maj. Francis Mauldin, Nicholas Ridgley, William Rumsey and John Veazey as commissioners.

f.92 (DSC02215)
==
Petition of Aaron Latham.* States that he owns land adjacent to the courthouse, but the markers for the land have "become blind and unknown" which prevents him from improving his lot. Asks court to have county surveyor reset and stake out the marks and also requests permission to clear land that is not yet possessed or cultivated by anyone. Court

orders a warrant to the county surveyor to lay out the courthouse land with Latham to erect locust posts at the corners.

Court adjourned until June session.

f.93 (DSC02215)

==

June Court 1726

Court convened 14 June 1726 at Elk River, continued until 18 June. Following commissioners present: Col. John Ward, Capt. James Alexander, Mr. Francis Mauldin, Col. Benjamin Pearce, Capt. Edward Jackson, Mr. Stephen Hollingsworth, Capt. Richard Thompson. Mr. Henry Ward, Mr. John Baldwin. Also present, John Smith, sheriff, and Stephen Knight, clerk.

Petition of Mathias Vanderheyden. States that he owns a parcel of the tract called The Rounds where the bounds are in decay. Asks court to form a commission to investigate and confirm the bounds. Court appoints Col. John Ward, John Baldwin, Nicholas Ridgley and William Rumsey as commissioners.

f.94 (DSC02216)

==

Petition of Evert Evertson.* States that Mary Lewes, widow and executrix of Edward Lewes, gave the care of his son, George Lewes, then a half-year old, to Evertson until age 21. The boy, now five years old, has been in Evertson's care since. Evertson is concerned that Mary Lewis may not have had legal authority to assign the boy to him and now asks the court to confirm the arrangement and formally bind the boy to him. Court orders that George Lewes be bound to Evert Evertson until age 21. Evertson is to teach him the trade of rope maker, to read, write and cypher (arithmetic) to the rule of three, bring him up in the Church of England and provide him with meat, drink, clothes and washing during his apprenticeship. When Lewis turns 21, he is to have his freedom and be given a new suit, hat, two shirts, shoes and stockings.

Petition of John Segars. States that he dwells near Bohemia ferry and asks to be given a license to keep a public house. Granted.

f.95 (DSC02216)

==

Petition of Edward Fottrell. States that he had practiced at the Chancery Court of Appeals and asks to be admitted as an attorney to practice in Cecil Court. Court so grants. Fottrell and John Alexander take the oaths prescribed by the act of assembly and both subscribe the Oath of Abjuration and Test.

Petition of Mathew Howard of Kent County. States that he owns a tract called Pullens Refuge on the north side of Sassafras River which shares a common bound with a tract called Painter's Rest. Asks that a commission be formed to verify and confirm the boundaries. Court appoints Col. Benjamin Pearce, John Baldwin, William Rumsey and Otho Othoson as commissioners.

Petition of William Borin. States that he has brought up an orphan named John Borin from infancy who is now of age to choose his guardian and has been brought to court to make his choice. William Borin also states that the boy has inherited a piece of land which is being wasted and destroyed by people taking its timber. Apparently legal guardianship gives Borin status to prosecute the offenders. Court acknowledges John Borin's right, and he chooses William Borin to be his guardian.

f.96 (DSC02217)

==

Petition of Samuel Chew of Ann Arundel County. States that he is the attorney in fact for the heirs of Richard Perry of London, deceased, who owned a tract called Perry Point at the mouth of the Susquehanna River, the first bounder tree of which is down and rotting. Asks that a commission be formed to verify and confirm the boundaries. Court appoints Capt. Edward Jackson, James Campbell, Stephen Onion and John Hamond as commissioners.

Petition of Jonathan Bavington, aged 18 years.* States that his deceased father, John Bavington, provided in his will that Jonathan "be free to act and do for himself at age eighteen" but that his mother put him into an indenture arrangement with John Stoopes, a cordwinder, until age 21. Stoopes afterwards moved to another county and put Bavington into other services not included in the indenture. Asks court to release him from the indenture. Court judges that he go free and be at his own disposal in accordance with his father's will.

f.97 (DSC02217)

==
Court adjourned until August session.

August Court 1726

Court convened 9 August 1726 at Elk River, continued until 12 August. Following commissioners present: Col. John Ward, Mr. Stephen Hollingsworth, Capt. Edward Jackson, Capt. James Alexander, Major Francis Mauldin, Mr. John Baldwin, Capt. Richard Thompson, Col. Benjamin Pearce, Mr. Henry Ward. Also present, John Smith, sheriff, and Stephen Knight, clerk.

Petition of Stephen Onion. States that he has built a mill on Rock Run and wishes to lay out a road to the ironworks. Asks for court's approval. Court grants petition, with Onion to cover expenses and "not to damnify any inhabitant thereabout."

f.98 (DSC02218)

==
Court adjourned until November session.

November Court 1726

Court convened 8 November 1726 at Elk River, continued until 15 November.* Following commissioners present: Col. John Ward, Mr. Henry Ward, Major Francis Mauldin, Mr. Stephen Hollingsworth, Capt. Edward Jackson, Mr. John Baldwin, Capt. James Alexander, Col. Benjamin Pearce, Also present, John Smith, sheriff, and Stephen Knight, clerk.

Petition of John Peterson.* States that he has for several years faithfully operated the Elk River ferry on behalf of Herman Kinkey, the ferry keeper appointed by the court. Peterson now requests that he be appointed ferry keeper for the next year which he says Kinkey has agreed to. Kinkey also signed the petition. Court approves Peterson as ferry keeper at usual allowance provided he posts recognizance bond of £20 sterling. Peterson posts bond with Thomas Biddle and Frances Foster as his security at £10 each.

f.99 (DSC02218)
===

Petition of James Van Bebber. States that in 1714 he had purchased a 270-acre parcel from his uncle, Mathias Van Bebber, adjoining Mathias's dwelling plantation, with the boundary marked by several trees notched 12 times under Mathias's direction. Yet "the said Mathias contrary to all the rules of justice and honour has of late caused all the trees to be cut down and destroyed in order to defeat your petitioner of his just claim." Asks court to form a commission to investigate and confirm the bounds. Court appoints Col. Benjamin Pearce, John Baldwin, Peter Bouchell and William Rumsey as commissioners.

Petition of Charles Rumsey. States that the road going by his fence is a problem and he would like to turn it in a way that will be as convenient to travelers as the present road. Court approves, with Rumsey to cover costs.

Petition of Joanna Damper. Asks for support from the county as a poor pensioner. Court allows her 1,500 lbs/tbco.

Petition of Sarah Prue. Asks for support from the county as a poor pensioner. Court allows her 1,200 lbs/tbco.

Petition of John Paine. Asks for support from the county as a poor pensioner. Court allows him 600 lbs/tbco.

f.100 (DSC02219)
===

Petition of James Christie, prisoner.* (See March Court 1725, f.91) States that he has been detained a prisoner of the sheriff as a debtor for lack of an affidavit or oath to his creditors in Baltimore County although he had complied with the requirements of the Act for Relief and Release of Poor Distressed Prisoners for Debt. He produces an affidavit from Dr. George Walker that Walker had delivered the required oath of Christie to his creditors, including Capt. Thomas Sheridan, Christopher Bandall and others, at last August Baltimore County Court, pledging that Christie's effects could be distributed among his creditors. Court orders that he be discharged from prison "whereof the Sheriff of Cecil County is to take notice."

Petition of Isaac Griffith. Asks for court to give license to keep a public house of entertainment. Court grants petition, Griffith to post a recognizance bond of £20 sterling. Peter Carick (?) and William Bristow pledge £10 each as his securities.

f.101 (DSC02219)

==
Petition of Thomas Paine. Asks for support from the county as a poor pensioner. Court allows him 200 lbs/tbco.

Petition of the inhabitants of north side of Sassafras River.* States that a road called the lower road was laid out near the coast some 40 years earlier when it was very thinly populated on the upper part of the north side. Most of the public places including the old courthouse were located near the mouth of the river on the north side at that time. The road was needed, but subsequent changes, including relocation of the courthouse to Elkton, render the road useless and its upkeep a burden. Ask to use two other roads and clear a new road from the head of Sassafras to Mr. Perry Phrisby's [Frisby's] where it will join the main road along the south side of Col. John Ward's plantation. Signed by Richard Houghton, Nathan Sapington, Otho Otheson, Thomas Beard, Oliver Caulk, Isaac Caulk, Neheimiah Martin, Nathaniel Hynion, Robert Nelding Sen., Robert Nelding, Jun., John Chamberling, Phillip Stoop, Mary Shore, Nicholas Dornel, Daniel Goo___, Robert Penington, James Bowers, John Aphey, Garret Vansandt, John Wotson, Walter Hill, Joseph Bawden, Dan Nolen, Nicholas Vanhoware?, William Savin, Sen., Thomas Savin, William Savin, Jun., Andrew Clements, Richard Bellew, Thomas Seerson, James Steel. Court orders that a main road be laid out and cleared according to directions of Col. John Ward and Col. Benjamin Pearce and that a special warrant be directed to the overseer of roads for North Sassafras Hundred.

f.102 (DSC92220)

==

Petition of John Dye.* States that the justices had for some time used the services of Sarah Dye (no relationship mentioned) for cleaning the courthouse. Asks that they extend the arrangement for another term. Court directs that Sarah Dye be paid 500 lbs/tbco for her work the past year but declines to renew the arrangement.

Petition of Ann Beaumont. States that she is "stricken in years and so far disabled in one of her arms that she is scarce able to keep herself and her child" without support from the county. Asks that she may take over the responsibilities of Mr. Dye for cleaning the courthouse at the same terms. Court approves, "she being an object of charity."

Petition of Ralph Rutter. States that he is a poor pensioner, having been lame for many years and has spent all that he has to maintain his family which has come to want. Asks court to make him levy free and to provide him with some allowance. Court directs that he be given an allowance of 1,000 lbs/tbco as an object of charity.

f.103 (DSC92220)

==

Petition of the vestry of St. Stephen's Parish. States that they had acquired a tract of some 300 acres from Col. William Ward for a glebe and that there was some concern about disputes of the boundaries. Asks court to form a commission to investigate and confirm the bounds of the tract. Court appoints Col. Benjamin Pearce, Nicholas Ridgley, Capt. Henry Rippon and William Rumsey as commissioners.

Petition of Mary Kettles. States that she had agreed to an indenture for her son, Joseph Seal, with Nathan Worley until age 21 under which Worley would teach the boy the trade of a house carpenter. She complains that Worley has not been teaching him any such trade and asks for some redress. Court adjudges that Joseph be discharged from his indenture to Worley with Worley consenting.

f.104 (DSC02221)

===

Petition of Elinor Ware.* States that the court had found Daniel Cook to have been the father of petitioner's unnamed child. Asks court to compel Daniel Cook pay her for the "complete maintenance" of the said child since birth. Court directs that Daniel Cook pay Elinor Ware 900 lbs/tobacco for "keeping the base born child begot on her body" and no more.

Court adjourned until March Session.

f.105 (DSC02221)

===

March Court 1726

Court convened 14 March 1726 at Elk River, continued until 17 March. Following commissioners present: Col. John Ward, Capt. James Alexander, Major Francis Mauldin, Mr. Henry Ward, Capt. Edward Jackson, Capt. Richard Thompson, Mr. Stephen Hollingsworth. Also present, John Smith, sheriff, and Stephen Knight, clerk.

Petition of Sarah Beaston, widow. States that she lives near a mill and that two roads going through her property—one to the mill and the other to the mill head—cause her great problems in having to erect fences by her cornfield. Asks that the roads can be turned in a less intrusive way. Court grants petition subject to her clearing a straight road from the west end of the race ground to the road to the head of the mill dam.

Petition of John Smith. Says that he owns a tract called Bormust (Warmust) on south side of Bohemia River near Scotchman's Creek, it being part of the estate of Col. Peter Hack of Virginia. The bounds of the tract are down and likely to be disputed. Smith asks that the court form a commission to investigate and verify the bounds. Court appoints Col. Benjamin Pearce, Nicholas Ridgley, John Baldwin and William Rumsey as commissioners.

f.106 (DSS02222)

===

Petition of Peter Bouchell. States that he owns a parcel of a large tract known as Labadies Land which is bounded by a path known as the Old Man's Path, now encumbered by fallen trees and in poor condition. Asks court to form a commission to investigate and establish the bounds. Court appoints Stephen Knight, John Campbell, John Ham and William Rumsey as commissioners.

f.107 (DSS02222)

=== =

Petition of George Child. States that he owns a 100-acre parcel of a tract called Shrewsbury, conveyed to him by William Cox, John Cox and Gilbert Cox, the boundaries of which may be disputed. Asks court to form a commission to investigate and verify the bounds. Court appoints Henry Ward, Capt. Henry Rippon, Nicholas Ridgley and John Penington as commissioners.

Petition of Howell James et al. States that James has built a mill on Bohemia Back Creek but that there is no public road leading to it. Asks court to order the overseer of the highway to have roads laid out "from the cross paths of Bohemia Manor to the mill or from the end of Col. Pearce's mill lane or further corner of Mullican's clear ground to James's mill." Court appoints William Bristow inspector to lay out a road from the cross paths to James's mill and orders a warrant to the overseer of that part of Bohemia Manor.

f.108 (DSS02223)

===

Petition of John Urmston. States that he has lost use of a pasture that became part of the glebe of St. Steven's Church and Rev. Sewell's plantation, and is now very burdened by having to fence a field with several roads through it, thus requiring multiple gates and much loss of pasture. Asks that the several roads be combined into one, with the Irish Road from White Marsh and Sassafras joining the road from the church to Capt. Rippon's mill and the road toward John Veazey's at corner of the field. Court declines to order roads be combined into one but approves rerouting them to reduce the gates required to three: one to White Marsh road, one to the ferry and one to Rippon's mill.

f.109 (DSS02223)

===

Petition of Joseph Clerk.* States that when his wife was in a sick and weak state in 1722, and in his absence, she put her son, Kelly Warren, then about five years old, into an indenture agreement with Enoch Enochson through the age of 21. Clerk says that he was a servant of John Coppon at the time and not advised of the agreement; he considers that it is illegal and asks the court to make judgment on it. Court judges that Joseph and his wife take custody of Kelly Warren and order Enoch Enochson to bring the said boy into June Court.

Petition of James Husbands. States that the boundaries of a tract he owns called Mount Pleasant on a branch of Sassafras Creek are decayed and some of the land is now claimed by other surveys. Asks court to form a commission to investigate and verify the bounds. Court appoints Col. Bayard, William Rumsey, Nathaniel Hynson and Otho Othoson as commissioners.

f.110 (DSC02224)

===

Petition of Henry Ward. Owns a tract called Long Acre, the bounds of which are decayed. Requests a commission be formed to investigate and confirm the bounds. Court appoints William Rumsey, John Camble, Thomas Rice and Peter Bouchell as commissioners.

Court adjourned until next session.

June Court 1727

Court convened 13 June 1727, at Elk River, continued until 17 June. Following commissioners present: Col. John Ward, Capt. Richard Thompson, Capt. Edward Jackson, Maj. Francis Mauldin, Capt. James Alexander, Mr. Henry Ward, Mr. Stephen Hollingsworth. Also present: John Smith, sheriff, and Stephen Knight, clerk.

f.111 (DSC02224)

==

Petition of Thomas Taylor, planter.* States that he has worked for several years as an inhabitant at the ironworks at Principio and was frequently pressed by travelers and workers to provide food and lodging. Requests a license to keep an ordinary. Court approves and requires that he post recognizance bond of £20. Cornelius Cormack and Solomon Rees pledge security of £10 each.

Petition of James Heath. States that there is confusion about location of a red oak forming a corner point between his property on tract called Heath's Outlet and land belonging to Matthew Howard of Kent County called Painter's Rest. Requests a commission be formed to investigate and confirm the bounds. Court appoints Col. Benjamin Pearce, Mr. John Baldwin, Mr. William Rumsey, Mr. Otho Othoson as commissioners.

f.112 (DSC02225)

==

Petition of Henry Reynolds. Complains that Henry Simmons, son of John Simmons, whom he took on as a cordwainer's apprentice for a six-year period was detained from returning to his service for unknown reasons. Requests court consider the case and confirm his contract or assign damages in recompense for the time he has given to Simmons. Court directs that Simmons be summoned to court.

Court adjourned until next session.

f.113 (DSC02225)

==

Petition of John Smith. Owns a tract called Warmust on the south side of Bohemia River. States that a previous commission did not know of several persons who could testify to the location of a bounder tree which is also a corner tree of a tract called Coaster's Harbor belonging to Matthias Van Bebber. Requests a commission be formed to investigate and confirm the bounds. Court appoints Col. Benjamin Pearce, Mr. John Baldwin, Mr. Nicholas Ridgley, Mr. William Rumsey as commissioners.

August Court 1727

Court convened 8 August 1727 at Elk River, continued until 11 August. Following commissioners present: Col. John Ward, Maj. Francis Mauldin, Capt. Edward Jackson, Mr. Stephen Hollingsworth, Capt. James Alexander, Col. Benjamin Pearce, Capt. Richard Thompson, Mr. Henry Ward. Mr. John Baldwin, Also present: John Smith, sheriff, and Stephen Knight, clerk.

f.114 (DSC02229)

==

Petition of James Calder. Who "having for some time applyed himself to the Study of the Law" requests that he be admitted as an attorney of the court. Granted. Calder takes the "usual" oaths and subscribes to the Oath of Abjuration.

Petition of William Shaw. Who had practiced law for some time in New Castle, Kent and Sussex counties requests that he be admitted as an attorney of the court. Granted. Shaw takes the "usual" oaths and subscribes to the Oath of Abjuration.

Petition of Ralph Rutter.* "Having been reduced to the utmost extremity" requests assistance in his "desperate condition." Rutter states that he had spent "the whole of his substance in looking for remedies" and found no relief for his unspecified affliction. Court consents to provide him 3,000 lbs/tbco "towards payment of a Doctor for his cure."

Court adjourned until next session.

f.115 (DSC02229)

==

November Court 1727

Court convened 14 November 1727 at Elk River, continued until 21 November. Following commissioners present: Col. John Ward, Mr. Henry Ward, Capt. Edward Jackson, Mr. John Baldwin, Capt. James Alexander, Mr. Stephen Hollingsworth, Maj. Francis Mauldin. Also present: John Smith, sheriff, and Stephen Knight, clerk.

Petition of Richard Touchstone, Sen. Planter, of Mount Ararat, aged 70 years, having served the county 43 years and "now almost past labour, having no help or assistance but his own hands, his wife also being old and crazy" requests that he be relieved of paying the levy or any taxes. Granted.

f.116 (DSC02230)
==
Petition of John Cox. States that James Husbands has retained custody of two orphans of Thomas Kurry((?)), deceased, and also their shares of their inheritance without having posted bond for security of same. The orphans are now of age to choose their guardians. Cox requests court summon orphans to make their choices and to make Husbands post bond. Court orders warrant be issued for Cox to bring the orphans into court and orders the sheriff to bring Husbands into court to answer charges.

Petition of Ralph Rutter, Jun. A poor pensioner who craves support. Court orders 2,000 lbs/tbco be allowed Rutter from current levy.

Petition of Sarah Prue. A poor pensioner who craves support. Court orders 1,000 lbs/tbco be allowed Prue from current levy.

Petition of Nicholas Sewall. Owns a tract called The Dividend at head of Bohemia River and requests that a commission be appointed to ascertain the boundaries before the persons who have knowledge of same "be called from this life … to the detriment of your petitioner." Court appoints Col. John Ward, Mr. John Baldwin, James VanBibber, Peter Bouchelle as commissioners.

f.117 (DSC02230)
==
Petition of Jeremiah Larkins.* Petitioner has "been in affliction" for a year and a half and been left destitute relying only on the mercy of God." He is now "going under the Doctor's hands but the Doctor is not willing to do anything to me unless that I get a note from under your Worships hands for an allowance in case of death." Court allows 1,000 lbs/tbco for

Dr. Rees with provision for an additional consideration should a "perfect cure" be made.

f.118 (DSC02231)

===

Petition of Stephen Hollingsworth. Acting as attorney for Charles Carroll, Esq., of Annapolis, states that Carroll owns the following properties in Cecil County where boundaries are decaying: Kellavelly (Killavilly, 200 acres), Darrow (350 acres), Deer Hill (50 acres), Derry Keell (Derry Heel, 1,900 acres), Forrall(?) (800 acres). Requests that a commission be established to inquire into their boundaries. Court appoints Mr. Thomas Johnson, Mr. John Smith, Mr. James Alexander, Maj. Francis Mauldin as commissioners.

Petition of John Hyland, Jun. States that he lives at one of the points of Bohemia Ferry that is much oppressed by travelers and requests that he be granted a license to operate a public house. Granted.

Petition of John Peterson who has operated the ferry at Elk River for some years and needs to purchase a new boat to continue the service. Requests allowance for same. Court grants request and provides allowance for Peterson to continue as ferryman for the next year.

f.119 (DSC02231)

===

Petition of John Veazey, owner of the greater part of a tract called Essex Lodge, situated on Scotchman's Creek, formerly Omealy Creek. Requests that commissioners be appointed to depose "sundry old persons" concerning the boundaries. Court appoints Col. Benjamin Pearce, Mr. William Rumsey, Mr. Henry Ward and Mr. John Penington as commissioners.

Petition of Joanna Dempier. Craves support as a poor pensioner. Court allows her 500 lbs/tbco from current levy.

Petition of Henry Hendrickson. States that when he served as a constable in 1725, he refunded Mr. Ridgley for an overcharge in the levy in the amount of 94 lbs/tbco. Asks to be reimbursed. Granted.

Court adjourned until next session.

==

March Court 1727
Court convened 12 March 1727 at Elk River, continued until 16 March. Following commissioners present: Col. John Ward, Capt. Edward Jackson, Maj. Francis Mauldin, Mr. James Alexander, Col. Benjamin Pearce, Mr. Henry Ward. Also present: Mr. John Baldwin, sheriff, and Stephen Knight, clerk.

Petition of Col. John Ward. Owns a tract called Greenfield where the beginning tree is decayed. Requests court to appoint a commission to investigate. Court appoints Col. Benjamin Pearce, Maj. John Dowdall, Mr. William Rumsey and Mr. Otho Othoson as commissioners.

==

Petition of John Wattson. States that he took into his house a poor woman named Mary Rafe "very unwell and stone blind" although he had a wife and children that he could barely support. Requests assistance from the county to provide support for the woman. Court finds that Wattson should continue to keep the woman until November court at which time they will consider some allowance.

==

Petition of John Baldwin, gent. Owns a 240-acre tract called MacGregory's Delight. States that the beginning tree is not well defined in the survey and requests commission to investigate. Court appoints Col. John Ward, Col. Benjamin Pearce, Mr. William Rumsey and Mr. Otho Othonson as commissioners.

Petition of John Smith, lately sheriff of Cecil County. States that former prisoner William Burton was released according to Act of Assembly for the Relief of Poor Prisoners and surrendered all his estate rights and credits to the court. Smith asks that he be given his proportionate share of these goods because of amounts due him as proved in documents filed with the court. Court approves.

f.123 (DSC02233)

==

Petition of Thomas John.* States that Jonathan Clark died intestate in the house of Thomas Preist (Preis) and left an orphan son now kept by Preist by court order. John states that the boy is subjected to "barbarous usage … beyond the dictates of Christianity" and that Clark also left goods and chattles now held by Preist for which he has not given an account. Requests court to intercede on behalf of the "poor forlorn child who hath no friend nor relations to see him righted." Court directs warrant to constable of Susquehanna Hundred to "bring the body of Thomas Preis & the orphan mentioned" into court this session. Nothing further on how the matter was resolved.

Petition of George Robinson. States that he rents land of Stephen Hollingsworth's plantation, which lies along an unspecified public road and requests a license to operate a public house on the property. Court grants request subject to recognizance bond of £20 sterling; John Smith and Robert Holy pledge as securities for Robinson at £10 each.

f.124 (DSC02234)

==

Petition of William Humphries.* States that he was committed by the court to John Smith, then sheriff of Cecil County, "as being a criminal servant to John Higginson of Kent Island." He was delivered as such, then bought from Higginson, but petitioner doesn't "consider himself servant any ways to the said Higginson or any other person." Petitioner requests that court require Smith or Higginson to make their claims against him in court. Court finds that the time he has served Smith since 17 May 1726 should be sufficient to satisfy the judgment against him "toward his fourfold & fees," but without court records at hand, final judgment is deferred to June court at which time Humphries is to produce the judgment and account of the fees.

Petition of John Campbell and John Veazey. Petitioners own the major part of a tract called The Dividing on which the beginning tree is decayed.

66

Request a commission be appointed to examine the site and confirm boundaries. Court appoints Mr. Henry Ward, Mr. William Rumsey, Mr. John Baldwin and Capt. Henry Rippon as commissioners.

f.125 (DSC02234)
===

Petition of Cornelius Tobye. States that he is now settled on land of Col. Pearce at head of Bohemia River along a public road and requests a license to keep an ordinary. Court approves subject to recognizance bond of £20 sterling; Matthias Van Bebber and John Ward pledge security of £10 each.

Petition of Peregrine Frisby. Owns a tract called Frisby's Meadows on the "draughts of Sassafras River" where the boundaries have become dubious, particularly the beginning tree which is also the second bounder of a tract called Greenfield. Requests a commission be formed to investigate the bounds. Court appoints Col. Benjamin Pearce, Mr. John Baldwin, Mr. William Rumsey, Mr. Otho Otheson as commissioners.

Court adjourned until next session.

f.126 (DSC02235)
===

May Court 1728
Court convened 6 May 1728. Commissioners not listed

Petition of Ann Toston (Thurston), an aged woman. States that she had worked for Clam Barkston and after his decease for his widow, now also deceased, but after much trouble has not obtained any payment for her work from the administrator of their estates. Requests that court order the administrators to pay her wages. Account entered itemizing 600 lbs/tbco for six months work in 1717 and £1/13/4 for four months work in 1722; attested by Roger Woolston. Court orders Col. Ephraim Augustine Herman, administrator of Clam Barkston's estate, to pay Toston 600 lbs/tbco.

Petition of John Carnan. States that he purchased a servant of Capt. Stone, claimed to be indentured but actually a convict and that Stone has now left the province. Requests the court's consideration. Court finds that the servant, William Cawdor, is "deemed and adjudged a convicted person."

f.127 (DSC02235)

===

Petition of Phillip Stoops and Nicholas Dorrell. Petitioners own a tract called Rook and Pill on Sassafras River where some bounder trees are decayed. Requests a commission be formed to investigate and confirm the bounds. Court appoints Maj. John Dowdall, Henry Ward, John Veazey and John Penington as commissioners.

Petition of Aron Latham, keeper of an ordinary. Notes that the Act of Assembly concerning ordinaries has expired but that he still has liquors and other ordinary accommodations. Requests that county allow him to "continue ordinary keeping according to the laws & customs of England." Court approves, subject to recognizance bond of £20 sterling; Richard Thompson and William Sinclair pledge security of £10 each.

Court adjourned until June session.

f.128 (DSC02236)

===

June Court 1728

Court convened 11 June 1728 at Elk River, continued until 14 June. Following commissioners present: Col. John Ward, Mr. Stephen Hollingsworth, Col. Benjamin Pearce, Maj. Francis Mauldin, Capt. Edward Jackson, Mr. Henry Ward, Capt. Richard Thompson. Also present: Mr. John Baldwin, sheriff, and Stephen Knight, clerk.

Petition of Joshua George.* At request of Edward Jennings, the petitioner, an attorney of the court, brought a case against Col. John Ward, one of the justices of the court, which also includes John Coppin, William Sinclair, Thomas Jones, George Veazey, Henry Ward, Josiah Sutton and Peter Bayard, gentlemen. Petitioner obtained a favorable verdict for his client for damages and cost. Subsequently Col. Ward wrote several persons, including some on this bench, reflecting on the petitioner's capacity, referring to him as villain, rascal and base fellow. Petitioner expresses hope

that his clients and the court bench will not be prejudiced by such insinuations and asks court to resolve that an attorney of this court not receive
such usage especially from a magistrate acting pursuant to his duty. After
consideration, the court states that it "is of the opinion that the petitioner has done nothing but his duty in that affair mentioned in the said petition."

f.129 (DSC02236)
==
Petition of Neal Cook.* States that when he formerly lived in Pennsylvania he took a male child named William Rutledge, about three months
old, the son of William Rutledge, into his care. That was about 12 to 13
years ago and the child has since become as one of his family. About eight
years ago Cook moved to Cecil County. In the years since he has brought
up and maintained the child as his own and has not heard from the parents nor knows where they are. Requests the court declare the boy an
orphan so he may be bound to him as one of his own family until of age.
Court agrees and binds William Rutledge to Neal Cook until of age. Cook
is to instruct him in farming and provide for him during his apprenticeship, to teach him "to read, write and cypher as far as Rule of Three, instruct him in the Protestant religion" and provide him with appropriate
clothing and a breeding mare at the completion of his term.

f.130 (DSC02237)
==
Court adjourned until next session.

August Court 1728
Court convened 13 August 1728 at Elk River, continued until 17 August.
Following commissioners present: Col. John Ward, Capt. Edward Jackson,
Col. Benjamin Pearce, Capt. Richard Thompson, Mr. Henry Ward, Maj.
Francis Mauldin and Mr. Stephen Hollingsworth. Also present: Mr. John
Baldwin, sheriff, and Stephen Knight, clerk.

f.131 (DSC02237)
==
Petition of Edward Buttler, apprenticed to Louis England to be taught the
trade of a millwright. States that England is now deceased and 11 months

remain of his agreed four-year apprenticeship. Buttler further states that the administrators of England's estate refuse to teach or support him and no one claims him. Requests court to give him liberty to seek his own living. Court rules that since no one appeared against him, petition is granted.

Petition of Peter Bouchell, David Lawson, Arnold Bassett, James Bayard and Benjamin Sluyter, inhabitants at head of Bohemia. Describe poor state of the road from Great House mill to Col. Pearce's mill and requests court to direct overseer of Bohemia Hundred to reroute the road over a suggested better path. Court approves and appoints Peter Bouchell, David Lawson, James Van Bebber and Benjamin Sluyter as inspectors to ensure road is properly laid out.

f.132 (DSC02238)
===

Petition of Augustine Thompson of Queen Anne's County. Owns a tract called Middle Plantation on north side of Sassafras River where bounder trees are decayed. Requests a commission be formed to investigate and confirm the bounds. Court appoints Col. John Ward, William Rumsey, Maj. John Veasey and John Penington as commissioners.

Petition of John Dowdall. Owns a tract called None So Good In Finland, lying at the head of Back Creek on north side of Sassafras River, where boundaries are uncertain. Requests a commission be formed to investigate and confirm the bounds. Court appoints Col. John Ward, William Rumsey, Maj. John Veasey and John Penington as commissioners..

Court adjourned until next session.

f.133 (DSC02238)
===

November Court 1728

Court convened 12 November 1728 at Elk River, continued until 16 November. Following commissioners present: Col. John Ward, Capt. Edward Jackson, Col. Benjamin Pearce, Capt. Richard Thompson, Capt. Edward Jackson, Maj. Francis Mauldin, Mr. Stephen Hollingsworth. Also present: Mr. John Baldwin, sheriff, and Stephen Knight, clerk.

70

Petition of Thomas John, farmer of Susquehanna Hundred. States that he had sold a servant man to John Pigot but the constable for the hundred listed the servant as a taxable to the petitioner's account. Petitioner refused to pay the tax, for which he was fined. Petitioner states that he will pay the tax but asks that the fine be dropped. Granted.

Petition of John Peterson, ferryman on Elk River. "Having with the utmost diligence kept and attended the ferry on Elk River the year past and having furnished himself with a very good new boat," petitioner requests he be allowed to keep the ferry for another year. Court approves Peterson to continue at the "usual allowance" until the next November court.

f.134 (DSC02239)
==

Petition of Ann Thurston. States she has lived in the county 29 years and been faithful to the country but now is aged and has lost the use of her eyes and hands and cannot maintain herself. Requests the court provide some support for her. Court allows 500 lbs/tbco from current levy.

Petition of Sarah Prue, poor pensioner. Court allows her 1,000 lbs/tbco from current levy.

Petition of the vestry of North Elk Parish, Richard Dobson, register.* States that the parish and churchyard are "very much out of repair" and requests that an assessment of 5 lbs/tbco be made on each taxable parishioner. Granted.

f.135 (DSC02239)
==

Petition of the vestry of St. Stephen's Parish, William Veasey, register. Requests an assessment of 5 lbs/tbco be made on each taxable in the parish. Granted.

Petition of Hugh Wattson. Owns a tract called Bancks on south side of Little Bohemia River the bounds of which are decayed, particularly the second bounder tree. Requests a commission be formed to investigate and confirm the bounds. Court appoints Col. Benjamin Pearce, Col. Ephraim Augustine Herman, Henry Ward, James Van Bebber as commissioners.

Petition of John Yorkson, Thomas Beard and Thomas Bowyer. Petitioners own a tract called Roundstone on Northeast River containing 300 acres, the bounds of which are decayed. Request a commission be formed to investigate and confirm the bounds. Court appoints Maj. Francis Mauldin, Edward Johnson, John Copson, Thomas Johnson as commissioners.

Court adjourned until next session.

f.136 (DSC02240)

===

March Court 1728 Court convened 11 March 1728 at Elk River, continued until 15 March.

Following justices present: Maj. Francis Mauldin, Mr. Henry Ward, Capt. Edward Jackson, Capt. James Alexander, Capt. Richard Thompson. Also present: John Baldwin, sheriff, and Stephen Knight, clerk.

Petition of Joseph Seely, who lives on "a common road." Requests a license to keep a public ordinary. Court approves, subject to posting security. No amount or guarantors mentioned.

Petition of Martin Alexander.* States that a judgment was rendered against him in favor of James Van Bebber for considerably more than was actually due. Requests that his case be "heard in equity" and that an attorney be assigned to manage his case "according to the rules of Chancery." Court appoints James Calder to represent him "so far as lays within the jurisdiction of this Court."

Court adjourned until next session.

f.137 (DSC02240)

===

June Court 1729

Court convened 10 June 1729 at Elk River, continued until 13 June.* Following Justices present: Col. John Ward, Mr. Stephen Hollingsworth, Capt. Edward Jackson, Capt. James Alexander, Maj. Francis Mauldin, Mr. Henry Ward. Also present: John Baldwin, sheriff, and Stephen Knight, clerk.

Petition of Jane Barry, on behalf of her son Joseph Williams.* Complains that a certain John Williams unjustly detains her son as a servant under pretense of a sale for £3/12/4 from petitioner. She states that she has no power to make such an agreement and would not do so in any case. Barry also states that John Williams keeps her son confined so that he cannot come to court himself. Requests court to order John Williams and her son be brought to court to answer her complaint. Court orders a summons be directed to the constable of Susquehanna Hundred to bring John Williams and Joseph Williams into court this session.

Petition of Robert Remington, Jun., planter. Owns a tract called Buntington on north side of Sassafras River on which the bounds are decayed. Requests a commission be formed to investigate and confirm the bounds. Court appoints Col. John Ward, Henry Ward, John Veazey, Mr. Robert Thompson as commissioners.

f.138 (DSC02241)
==

Petition of Howard James. States that he lives at and keeps Back Creek mill on main road from Elk River to Bohemia Ferry and is frequently pressed by travelers and strangers for accommodations. Requests that he be permitted to keep a "house of entertainment." Court approves. No further conditions.

Petition of Mary Whitton. States that sometime ago Francis Mauldin had left improved land with a house, livestock and other chattels to her in an "instrument of writing" which is kept by Nicholas Bailey and not given to her, contrary to her wishes. Requests that court appoint her uncle Richard Whitton as her guardian and place whatever belongs to her in his hands. Court appoints Richard Whitton as guardian to Mary Whitton.

Court adjourned until next session.

==

August Court 1729

Court convened 12 August 1729 at Elk River, continued until 16 August. Following commissioners present: Col. John Ward, Capt. Richard Thompson, Maj. Francis Mauldin, Capt. James Alexander, Capt. Edward Jackson. Also present: Mr. John Baldwin, sheriff, and Stephen Knight, clerk.

Petition of John Scott. Requests he be admitted as an attorney to the court. Granted. Scott takes the "usual oaths" and subscribes to the Oath of Abjuration.

Petition of Col. John Ward. Petitioner owns a tract called Colleton where bounders are decayed. Requests a commission be formed to investigate and confirm the bounds. Court appoints Henry Ward, Robert Thompson, Mr. Cosden, Henry Penington, Jun., as commissioners.

Court adjourned until next session.

==

November Court 1729

Court convened 11 November 1729 at Elk River, continued until 18 August. Following Commissioners present: Col. Benjamin Pearce, Mr. Stephen Hollingsworth, Capt. Edward Jackson, Capt. Richard Thompson, Capt. James Alexander, Mr. William Rumsey, Mr. Henry Ward, Mr. John Copson. Also present: John Baldwin, sheriff, and Stephen Knight, clerk.

Petition of John Paine, a poor pensioner. Allowed 650 lbs/tbco from present levy.

Petition of the inhabitants of Susquehanna Hundred.* States that the road from John Dawson's in Nottingham to Susquehanna Lower Ferry is now blocked off by new settlers and they are not allowed to pass through. Requests that court order a new road be laid out in the most convenient way. Signed by Samuel White, Enoch Enochs, Robert Hand, James Dillon, Joshua Richardson, John Kersey, Samuel Brice, Cornelius

McCormack, Henry Bowen, John Sortill, Jonathan Hartshorrne, John Chenoweth, Lazarus James, Mathew Acth, John Piggot. Court grants petition and appoints Cornelius McCormack as overseer.

f.141 (DSC02266)
===
Petition of inhabitants of Susquehanna Hundred. States that increasing population has led to the need for a new road from the church road by the Indian town called Poppometto(?) to where it joins the road leading to the Quaker Meeting House at the west end of Nottingham. Signed by Enoch Enochs, Robert Hand, James Dillon, Joshua Richardson, John Kersey, John Piggott, Samuel Brice, Cornelius McCormack, Henry Bowen, John Sortill, Jonathan Hartshorne, John Chenoweth, Lazarus James, Matthew Acth. Court grants petition and appoints Cornelius McCormack as overseer.

Petition of Hannah Johnson. Complains that she is unlawfully detained by Miles Godman, innkeeper, as a servant. Requests court to summon Godman to explain his rights. Court orders a summons for Miles Godman who appears in court. After hearing both sides the court rules that the indenture of the petitioner to Robert Anderson is valid and she is to serve "the said assignee" accordingly.

f.142 (DSC02267)
===
Petition of inhabitants of New Munster.* States the great need for repairing the road from New Munster to Head of Elk River and requests that an overseer be appointed. Signed by James Alexander, James Alexander, Moses Alexander and James Alexander. Court approves and appoints James Alexander, tanner, as overseer.

Petition of John Oliver, planter. States that he is very ancient and his wife is "past labour" and they have a great family. Requests that he be taken off the levy. Court grants petition and allows him 150 lbs/tbco from the current levy.

f.143 (DSC02267)

==

Petition of inhabitants of St. Stephen's Parish. States that a road is much needed from Brapons(?) Point on Bohemia River to Giddion Pearce's ferry at Sassafras. Request that proper person be appointed to construct the road. Signed Cornelius McCormack, Thomas Bard, Thomas Harper, Nicholas Hyland, Isaac Miller, Hugh Terry, Richard Thompson, John Campbell, Thomas Jones, John Prise, George Child, John Clark, Henry Penington, William Ward, Isbell Van Burcheloe, William Penington, Nicholas Ridgley, James Collings, Robert Penington, Sen., John Coxell, John Lusby, William Rumsey, Thomas Chenoweth, John Baldwin, John Copon, Robert Storey, Benjamin Slyter, William Crow, Amon Latham, John Hollett, John Crear(?). Court approves and appoints William Rumsey and John Baldwin as inspectors of the road with "full power to direct & order that the respective overseers of the several hundreds see the said road performed."

Petition of Walter Cockrell.* States that he has lost the use of his limbs and suffers from other distempers so is utterly unable to support himself. Requests the court provide some support for him. Court declares that Cockrell henceforth be levy free and allows him 250 lbs/tbco.

Petition of Cornelius VanSandt. States that he was charged for three taxables the past year but had only two. He appealed to the sheriff but could get no redress. Court orders that he be given credit for 109 lbs/tbco from present levy.

f.144 (DSC02268)

==

Petition of the vestry of St. Stephen's Parish, William Veazey, register. Requests an assessment of 5 lbs/tbco be made on each taxable in the parish. Granted.

Petition of Alphonse Cosden. Petitioner owns a tract called Warmust on south side of Bohemia River, adjacent to tract called Coaster's Harbor and formerly property of Peter Hack of Virginia, the bounds of which are much decayed. Requests a commission be formed to investigate and confirm the bounds. Court appoints Col. Benjamin Pearce, William Rumsey, John Baldwin and Col. Nicholas Ridgley as commissioners.

f.145 (DSC02268)

===

Court adjourned until next session.

March Court 1729

Court convened 10 March 1729 at Elk River, continued until 16 March.
Following commissioners present: Col. Benjamin Pearce, Mr. Stephen Hollingsworth, Capt. Edward Jackson, Mr. William Rumsey, Capt. Richard Thompson, Mr. John Copson, Mr. Henry Ward, Capt. James Alexander. Also present: John Baldwin, sheriff, and Stephen Knight, clerk.

f.146 (DSC02269)

===

Petition of Col. Ephraim Augustine Herman. Petitioner owns Bohemia Manor where boundaries of a 500-acre parcel conveyed first to Richard Bringham, then to Robert French are now decayed. Requests a commission be formed to investigate and confirm the bounds. Court appoints William Rumsey, John Campbell, John Hamm and Dr. Peter Bouchell as commissioners.

Petition of Daniel Noolan. States that the road by his plantation would be more commodious by turning it a shorter and leveler way. Noolan offers to make necessary changes at his charge. Granted.

f.147 (DSC02269)

===

Petition of William Rumsey. States that the road by his plantation is inconvenient to him and could be made more commodious by turning it a different way. Rumsey offers to make necessary changes at his charge. Granted.

Petition of sundry inhabitants of Susquehanna.* States that Thomas Cresap serves as the ferryman for Upper Susquehanna ferry and that access to the ferry is much inconvenienced by lack of an access road running from the ferry to Octoraro Road near the lately built chapel. The present road runs by various properties in the surrounding area and gets rerouted arbitrarily by the respective owners. Requests that persons be ap-

77

pointed to lay out a new road and make recommendation to the court. Signed by Stephen Onion, William Husband, John Chenoweth, John Piggott, William Arindell, Nicholas Arindell, John Alling, Abraham Watson, Cornelius Cormack, Samuel Young, William Bayley, John Mead, John Pidcock, Joseph Young, Court agrees and appoints John Hamond and Stephen Onion as inspectors to supervise laying out of new road.

Petition of Nathan Phillips.* Complains that his servant, George Williams, has frequently run off, incurring extravagant charges. Phillips presents an itemized list including £3/8/3 in charges made at New Castle, Welch Tract and Chester; also cites 29 days of absence from work. Requests redress from the court on these items. Court accepts Phillips' case and orders that Williams serve an additional six months beyond his contracted time.

f.148 (DSC02270)
==
Petition of Dominic Carroll.* Owns a tract called The Addition on south side of Bohemia River where bounds are old and decayed. Requests a commission be formed to investigate and confirm the bounds. Court appoints Col. Benjamin Pearce, William Rumsey, Alphonse Cosden and John Veasey as commissioners.

Court adjourned until next session.

June Court 1730
Court convened 9 June 1730 at Elk River, and adjourned until 21 July. Following commissioners present: Col. Benjamin Pearce, Mr. John Hamond, Capt. Edward Jackson, Capt. James Alexander Mr. Stephen Hollingsworth, Mr. Henry Ward, Capt. Richard Thompson, Mr. William Rumsey, Mr. John Copson. Also present: John Baldwin, sheriff, and Stephen Knight, clerk. No business recorded for 9 June.

f.149 (DSC02270)
==
Court adjourned until 3rd Tuesday in July. Reconvened 21 July 1730.

Petition of James Cronkelton.* States that a youth named Francis Boie had signed as an indentured servant to him for five years on 6 June 1729, with the approval of his family, but that the word "twenty" had been omitted in the date. Now the youth is detained by a Thomas Reynolds under pretense that the original agreement has long since expired. Court finds that the indenture was in fact entered into in 1729 and the youth should serve Cronkelton for five years and nine months from that time. Cronkelton is to provide him sufficient meat, drink, lodging and apparel, teach him a weaver's trade and at the end of his term provide him with a loom and two suits. Reynolds to pay Cronkelton for his legal costs.

Petition of Abraham Darlington, on behalf of Benedict Oram, son of Jonas Oram, deceased. Complains that "a certain [John] Justice of this County" administered the estate of the said Jonas Oram and that a considerable balance remained. Requests that the court oblige Justice to post security for the orphan's estate. Court concurs and issues summons for John Justice to appear in Court.

f.150 (DSC02271)
==
Petition of George Child and John Chambers. Petitioners state that they had some time earlier been bound in the amount of £10 each for the good behavior and appearance of a certain Margret Haddock. There follows a confusing statement asserting that the pledged security was forfeited through the ignorance of the petitioners but that the Governor would "remit" the sums if the court certifies the truth of their assertions about no prosecutions of the said woman. Statement of Benedict Leonard Calvert is attached: "I do hereby in his Lordship's name remit the forfeitures on the recognizances herein mentioned & will not they be levied."

Court adjourned until next session.

f.151 (DSC02271)
==
August Court 1730
Court convened 11 August 1730 at Elk River, continued until 14 August. Following commissioners present: Col. Benjamin Pearce, Mr. John Copson, Capt. Edward Jackson, Mr. William Rumsey, Capt. Richard Thompson, Mr. John Hamond, Capt. James Alexander, Mr. Henry Ward,

Capt. Thomas Colvill. Also present: John Baldwin, sheriff, and Stephen Knight, clerk.

Petition of Edward Larramore. Petitioner owns a tract of land called [omitted] where bounds are decayed. Requests a commission be formed to investigate and confirm the bounds. Court appoints Col. Benjamin Pearce, William Rumsey, Nicholas Ridgley and Alphonse Cosden as commissioners.

Court adjourned until next session.

f.152 (DSC02272)

==

November Court 1730
Court convened 10 November 1730 at Elk River, continued until 14 November. Following commissioners present: Col. Benjamin Pearce, Capt. Thomas Colvill, Capt. Edward Jackson, Mr. John Copson, Capt. James Alexander, Mr. John Hamond, Mr. William Rumsey. Also present: John Baldwin, sheriff, and Stephen Knight, clerk.

Petition of Ann Thurston, a poor pensioner. Requests support from the county. Court allows her 500 lbs/tbco from present levy.

Petition of Nicholas Dorrell and Phillip Stoops. Petitioners own a tract called Rook and Pill on the north side of Sassafras River, the second bounder of which is said to stand at a point called by the now-obsolete name Jones Point. Request a commission be formed to investigate and confirm the bounds. Court appoints William Rumsey, Nicholas Ridgley, Alphonse Cosden and John Baldwin as commissioners.

f.153 (DSC02272)

==

Petition of Henry Penington. Petitioner owns a tract called Happy Harbour on Sassafras River, the bounds of which are much decayed. Requests a commission be formed to investigate and confirm the bounds. Court appoints William Rumsey, Nicholas Ridgley, Alphonse Cosden and John Baldwin as commissioners.

Petition of John Coppen. Petitioner owns a tract called Silvanes Folly on north side of Sassafras River and bordering on Hack's Creek. Requests a commission be formed to investigate and confirm the bounds. Court appoints William Rumsey, Nicholas Ridgley, Alphonse Cosden and John Baldwin as commissioners.

f.154 (DSC02273)

==

Petition of Matthew Wallace.* States that he has been an inhabitant of the county for a considerable number of years and "contributed unto all public payments" but now is almost 80 years old and having no certain habitation is unable to pay his levy, Asks that Court allow him such alms as they seem meet. Court allows him 100 lbs/tbco from present levy.

Petition of John Paine, poor petitioner. Requests support from the county. Court allows him 500 lbs/tbco.

Petition of Dominic Carroll and Robert Pennington. Petitioners state that a main road passing through their plantations at the head of Bryant's Creek is now very much unused because a newer road now goes through Carroll's land. Request the court's permission to no longer maintain the road. Granted.

f.155 (DSC02273)

==

Petition of John Watson. States that he had taken care of a pensioner of the county known as Mary Rose, a blind woman, providing her with food, lodgings, washing and mending since 2 March. He has had a difficult time with her and requests the county to provide support. The court allows 600 lbs/tbco from current levy for eight months' accommodation.

Petition of Solomon Bowen.* States he was born in Cecil County, and "at the pleasure of Almighty God entirely deprived of his sight & thereby incapable of getting his living & being entirely destitute of all necessaries of life, both food and raiment." Requests support from the county. Court allows him 600 lbs/tbco as a poor pensioner from present levy.

Petition of Sapience Harrison. Complains that Daniel Hall, now a prisoner of the sheriff, is an indentured servant to her but has absented himself and pretends to be under no obligation. Asks court to summon Hall to explain himself. Court directs that Hall be brought to court to answer her complaint.

f.156 (DSC02274)
==

Petition of Thomas Chesnall,* on behalf of himself and his children. States that he had formerly been a servant of John Stokes and was convicted of being lazy but was given a pardon by the late governor which reinstated him. The said John Stokes afterward sold him and his children to Jefferson George for a term of years not yet expired. Requests court to enquire by what right Stokes sold Chesnall and his children and how they are kept in servitude and slavery to Jefferson George. Court considers the premises and judges that the indenture is good for the term of 31 years "therein mentioned" and against his children until they are 21.

Petition of William Piles. States that he has been lame a long time and cannot pay for medical care. His family has nothing to subsist on and suffers greatly. Asks the court for support from the county. Court asks Dr. [Peter] Bouchelle to take Piles under his care and allows 500 lbs/tbco from the next levy to cover cost, "provided he perform a cure."

f.157 (DSC02274)
==

Petition of William Godment. Petitioner lives at Bohemia Ferry and has a "good flat and hands." Offers to keep the ferry for the ensuing year for 4,000 lbs/tbco which is "considerable lessening it" from previous charges. Court approves, requiring that Godment post appropriate security.

Petition of John Hallett, constable of Bohemia Manor Hundred. States that due to "a bad or careless scribe" two more taxables had been listed for the hundred than should have been and Hallett was required to pay for them, amounting to 250 lbs/tbco. Requests he be recompensed from the levy. Court allows him 140 lbs/tbco "being it appears the county profited by his mistake."

f.157 (sic) **(DSC02275)**

==

Petition of Joshua George. Petitioner owns a tract called Little Neck or Little Bohemia where bounders are decayed and other trees have been mis-marked. Requests a commission be formed to investigate and confirm the bounds. Court appoints Col. Benjamin Pearce, John Baldwin, William Rumsey and Alphonse Cosden as commissioners.

f.158 (DSC02275)

==

Petition of Obediah Obein. Petitioner "has been a dealer these several years" but is now 68 years old and "disabled in his limbs." His wife is even older and also subject to infirmities. Requests that he be made levy free for the rest of his life and be considered for support from the county. Court agrees to make him levy free and allows him 100 lbs/tbco.

Petition of Richard Dobson of the vestry of St. Mary's Church. States that the church is decayed and out of repair. Requests court to assess 8 lbs/tbco on each taxable parishioner. Granted. Court also allows him 250 lbs/tbco.

f.159 (DSC02276)

==

November Court 1730 adjourned to December

Petition of John Penington.* States that Jamin[?] Johnson, a stranger, came to his house this past September and was taken ill by "a bloody flux" from which he died. Penington incurred considerable expense for both the care and burial of Johnson, who was destitute. Requests court to provide some recompense from county levy.

Petition of John Campbell. Petitioner owns part of a tract called Thompson Town on east side of Elk River. Requests a commission be formed to investigate and confirm the bounds. Court appoints Capt. Thomas Colville, William Rumsey, Richard Thompson and John Baldwin as commissioners.

f.160 (DSC02276)

===

Petition of John McManus.* States that he had practiced law in several courts in Ireland "with some success." Requests to be admitted to practice in Cecil Court. Court grants petition. McManus takes "the usual oaths" and subscribes to the Oath of Abjuration.

Petition of Henry Penington. Petitioner owns a tract called Hack's Creek where boundaries are much decayed. Requests a commission be formed to investigate and confirm the bounds. Court appoints John Baldwin, William Rumsey, Nathaniel Hyland and Robert Thompson as commissioners.

Petition of John MacDougall.* Petitioner states that he "foolishly, rashly and unadvisedly incurred the displeasure of your worships" and is now required to become a servant to pay the fine. Asks for mercy and some reduction of the fine. Court remits half of the fine. Amount not stated.

f.161 (DSC02277)

===

Petition of Joseph Dowding. Petitioner who had practiced law for some time in Kent County requests to be admitted as an attorney in Cecil court. Court grants petition. Dowding takes "the usual oaths" and subscribes to the Oath of Abjuration.

Petition of Catherine Bryan.* Petitioner who "for a considerable time has labored under a violent malady that will in the end prove fatal" requests some support from the county. Court allows her 1,000 lbs/tbco as a poor pensioner from present levy.

Court adjourned until next session.

March Court 1730

Court convened 9 March 1730 at Elk River, continued until 13 March. Following commissioners present: Col. Benjamin Pearce, Mr. Henry Ward, Capt. Edward Jackson, Capt. Thomas Colville, Capt. Richard Thompson, Mr. William Rumsey, Mr. Stephen Hollingsworth, Mr. John Copson, Mr. John Hamond. Also present: John Campbell, sheriff, and Stephen Knight, clerk.

f.162 (DSC02277)

==

Petition of Dominic Carroll. States that the court had previously formed a commission to examine the bounds of his part of a property called The Addition. He also owns part of the adjacent property called Swan Harbor, the other parts of which belonged to John Pool who sold to Robert Crook and James Holloway. Requests a commission be formed to investigate and confirm the bounds of these properties. Court appoints Col. Benjamin Pearce, William Rumsey, Alphonso Cosden and John Veasey as commissioners.

Petition of Nicholas Ridgley, John Campbell, William Price, Richard Price, Hyland Price, Mary Panlon and Edward Harris. Petitioners live in Price's Neck from which a public road leads to an unspecified church. With the road being neglected for some years by its overseers, request that the court designate this road and the connecting road to Bohemia ferry as public roads to be properly repaired and maintained by the overseer of highways. Court grants petition and directs the petitioners to clear the said roads at their charge, which in the future will be maintained by the hundred's overseer of roads. Nicholas Ridgley and John Veazey designated inspectors of said roads.

f.163 (DSC02278)

==

June Court 1731

Court convened 8 June 1731 at Elk River, continued until 12 June. Following commissioners present: Capt. Edward Jackson, Capt. James Alexander, Mr. William Rumsey, Capt. Richard Thompson, Mr. John Copson Mr. Stephen Hollingsworth, Mr. Henry Ward, Mr. John Hamond. Also present: John Campbell, sheriff, and Stephen Knight, clerk.

Petition of Benjamin Stoops. States that he has "not been able to do a stroke of work for above twelve months" because of his "consumptive disposition" and cannot pay the doctor's bills. Requests that he be taken off the levy. Court allows him an unrecorded sum.

Petition of Jethro Brown and his wife Sarah, executrix of Nathan Baker, deceased. Petitioners complain that John Piddock, laborer, who had signed a five-year service agreement with Nathan Baker to pay off debts due to Baker, John Copson and others, had absented himself and could not be obliged to return and satisfy his obligation. Request court to summon Piddock to court to answer their complaint. Court directs that a summons be issued.

f.164 (DSC02278)
===

Petition of John Hack.* States that he has an affliction which makes him utterly unable to work. He has lived in the province for over 30 years, most of it in Cecil County but is now a pauper. Requests that court provide him some allowance. Court directs that he be provided 400 lbs/tbco in next levy.

Petition of Elizabeth Baker. Complains that she is claimed and detained by John Copson as a servant but that she is under no such obligation to him or anyone else. Requests the court to have Copson answer to her complaint and do justice as appropriate. Court judges that she is free from any indenture to Copson, based on court testimony given by John Darlington.

f.165 (DSC002279)
===

Petition of James Heath. Owns a tract called Heath's Fifth Parcel where the bounds are "somewhat doubtful." Requests a commission be formed to investigate and confirm the bounds of these properties. Court appoints Mr. William Rumsey, Richard Thompson, John Baldwin and Nicholas Ridgley as commissioners.

Petition of John Williams and other near inhabitants of Susquehanna Upper Ferry.* States that the ferry is much frequented by travelers from the lower part of the province to Philadelphia and that there is no good road from the ferry going that way. Requests court to have a road "cutt the nearest and best way from the ferry place towards Philadelphia so far as the jurisdiction of this Court at present doth extend." Signed by Robert Layor, David Layor, John McTyre, John Mitchell, John Williams, John Hamond, Robert Porter, John Bond, John Hunter, John McConell, Alexander McConell, David Creswell, Hugh Barry, John Macdanel, James Paulson, Henry Touchstone, Christopher Touchstone, James Bond, Benjamin Clease, Thomas Renshaw, Samuel Bishop. Court grants petition and directs that the road be cleared by the petitioners at their charge. No overseer appointed.

f.166 (DSC002279)

===

Petition of Samuel Chew, Sen., attorney for John Perry and other legatees of Col. Richard Perry, deceased. States that Col. Perry died in possession of a tract called Perry's Neck between Back Creek and Perry Creek on the Susquehanna River where the bounds are now decayed. Requests a commission be formed to investigate and confirm the bounds. Court appoints Capt. Japhel(?) Jackson, John Copson, John Hamond and Joseph Young as commissioners.

Petition of John Hamond, and other uppermost inhabitants of Cecil County on Susquehanna River.* States that Upper Ferry and Merchants mill at nearby Rock Run mark the northernmost navigable point up the Susquehanna for "boats of burden" to which tobacco can be rolled for shipping. Requests that a road be cleared from a place called Duck(?) Bottom to Rock Run mill and from there to Upper Ferry. Signed by John Hamond, Paul Paulson, John Williams, John Bass. Court grants petition and appoints Randall Death as overseer of the road.

f.167 (DSC02280)

===

Petition of Edward Larramore. Petitioner owns several tracts called Larramore's Enlargement, Larramore's Neck in Large and Larramore's Addition, the bounds of which are decayed. Requests a commission be formed to investigate and confirm the bounds of these properties. Court appoints Col. Benjamin Pearce, William Rumsey, Nicholas Ridgley and Alphonso Cosden as commissioners.

Court adjourned until next session.

August Court 1731

Court convened 10 August 1731 at Elk River, continued until 14 August. Following commissioners present: Col. Benjamin Pearce, Capt. Richard Thompson, Capt. Edward Jackson, Mr. William Rumsey, Capt. James Alexander, Capt. Thomas Colville, Mr. Henry Ward, Mr. John Hamond. Also present: John Campbell, sheriff, and Stephen Knight, clerk.

f.168 (DSC02280)

===

Petition of Robert Handy. States that he is 68 years old, "past my labour" and so poor that he can scarcely subsist. Requests that court make him levy free. Court allows him 10 lbs/tbco as a poor pensioner.

Petition of John Williams. Petitioner owns a tract called Anchor and Hope on the Susquehanna River the bounds of which are decayed. Requests a commission be formed to investigate and confirm the bounds. Court appoints Capt. Edward Jackson, John Cosden, Edward Johnson and Thomas Johnson as commissioners.

Petition of Richard Cleaver. States that he served Henry Penington as a servant but since the end of his term has not been able to work and "must inevitable perish" without some relief from the county. Court allows him 300 lbs/tbco from next levy as a poor pensioner.

Court adjourned until next session.

f.169 (DSC02281)

===

November Court 1731

Court convened 9 November 1731 at Elk River, continued until 16 November.* Following commissioners present: Col. Benjamin Pearce, Capt. Thomas Colvill, Capt. Edward Jackson, Mr. John Hamond, Mr. Henry Ward, Capt. James Alexander, Mr. William Rumsey, Mr. John Copson. Also present: John Campbell, sheriff, and Stephen Knight, clerk.

Petition of John Veazey. Owns two tracts called True Game and Manchester, the boundaries of which are decayed. Requests a commission be formed to investigate and confirm the bounds. Court appoints Nicholas Ridgley, Henry Ward, Alphonso Cosden and John Baldwin as commissioners.

Petition of Brigett Watson.* States that she is 61 years old and has lived in the county for 23 years. She is wholly destitute, has no husband, relations or friends, no estate or ability of body to labor. Begs to be considered an object of charity and be given support by the county. Court allows her 500 lbs/tbco from present levy as a poor pensioner.

f.170 (DSC02281)
==

Petition of John Hackett.* States that he has been reduced by several sicknesses to the last extremity and is incapable of providing for his subsistence. Begs to be considered an object of charity by the county. Court allows him 500 lbs/tbco from present levy as a poor pensioner.

Petition of Martin Richmond. States that he has lived in the county for 30 years and that he and his wife are now very ancient. He has been very lame for many years and incapable of laboring. Asks for support in paying the present levy and to be levy free in the future. Court allows him 100 lbs/tbco as a poor pensioner in the present levy.

f.171 (DSC02282)
==

Petition of sundry inhabitants of Milford Hundred. States that road from Elk River to Nottingham and the road from Elk River to Robert Hutton's divide a tract called White's Folly owned by Isaac Miller, and that both the said roads and the tract intersect the road from New Munster to Hollingsworth Mill and thence to Nottingham. The road from Elk River to Nottingham is therefore redundant and petitioners request that it may be taken from use as a road. Signed by John Lawson, Gideon Harper, Thomas Wallace, James Hobetts, John Finlay, Martin Cartmell, Hugh Lawson, John Hogshead, Morgan Patton. Moses Andrews, John Ritchey, Joseph Cougheran, Charles Cambel, Robert Ritchey, Andrew Wallace, Thomas Moore. Court grants petition.

Petition of James Earle, sheriff of Queen Ann's County, and George Symco. Petitioners own a tract called Anna Catherine's Neck, or Carpenter's Point, near the mouth of the Susquehanna River where the bounds may soon be "rendered precarious." Requests a commission be formed to investigate and confirm the bounds. Court appoints Capt. Edward Jackson, Mr. John Currier, Mr. Jethro Brown and Mr. Randall Death as commissioners.

f.172 (DSC02282)

==

Petition of the vestry of St. Mary Ann's Parish, Richard Dobson, register.* States that they have made repairs to the church and churchyard and have no funds to defray expenses for these and other needed repairs. Asks that an assessment of 4 lbs/tbco be levied on the taxable parishioners. Court approves an assessment of 2 lbs/tbco on the parishioners.

Petition of William Saving. States that the road from Head of Sassafras to Head of Bohemia and on to Philadelphia goes through his land and is troublesome in many places. If it could be extended along Bohemia Ferry road next to Thomas Beard's instead of turning at Daniel Noland's land it would be no longer but much better. Requests that court approve suitable changes in the path of the road. Court appoints Col. John Ward and Otho Othoson as inspectors to see if road may be laid out as proposed and report back by the adjourned Court. Any alterations to be made at the charge of the petitioner.

f.173 (DSC2283)

==

Petition of Thomas Davis and sundry other inhabitants of Sassafras.* States that the road from Head of Sassafras to the old courthouse at James Town goes through his land and has been very troublesome. The road is now little used since the courthouse has been relocated to Elk River and the ferry to Penington Point. The road could be continued by using the road leading from the church past petitioner's land and turned to the road from the church to James Town. Asks court to approve alterations as needed to be done at petitioners' charge. Signed by William Ward, Robert Money, John Roberts, James McManus, John Penington, Benjamin Bonitt, William Penington, Nathaniel Hynson, Phillip Stoops,

Benjamin Davis, Robert Penington, James Wroth, John Price, John Bateman, John Tree, William Foster, William Freeman, Jacob Freeman, Benjamin Hastehurst(?), John Johnes, Richard Heally, John Jackson, Thomas Tyland, John Kimber, Henry White, John Cox, John Morris, Henry Hendrickson, Thomas Wats, William Wats, James Husband, - Matts, Nathaniel Freeman, Benjamin Cox, John Dye, Christopher Denning, Thomas Ward, John Clark, Garret Otheson, William Whettham, George Hollen, John Collins, John Dykes, John Ward, Robert Mercer, Thomas Mercer, Sen., John Mercer, James Lattomus, Andrew Presler, Peter Wallace, Peter Humbers, Kinesen(?) Wroth, George Childs, John Welsh, Robert Porter, John Capen, Athey Capen, George Greenwood, John Chambers, David Young, William Freeman, Jun., Thomas Freeman, David Rees, John Gullet, Thomas Senerson, Henry Penington, Sen., Henry Penington, Jun., Thomas Jones, Tench Davis, William Biggs(?), Nicholas Dorrel, Jacob Ozier, Abraham Hollings, Robert Otheson, William Oldfield, Thomas Pearce, Thomas Beard, Richard Houghton, Richard Grace, Alexander Clemens, George Woodhill, James Collins, Daniel Benson, James Morgan, Jun., John Severson, Cornelius Clemens, Thomas Rodgers, Mathaias Persons, James Kimber, Thomas Kimber, James Morgan, Sen., Jeffry Senerson, Samuel Barnum, Rees Owing, John MacKleen, David Rise, William Hugg, Peter Severson, Edward Burk, Thomas Penington, Andrew Clements. Court grants petition.

f.174 (DSC2283)
==
Petition of Henry Penington, Jun. States that he has a storehouse and dwelling house at the ferry on north side of Sassafras River where many travelers pass by. Requests a license to keep a public house, tavern and ale house. Court grants petition subject to posting security as required by law. Penington enters into recognizance for £20, with John Campbell and Thomas Davis his securities at £10 each.

Court adjourned until next session.

March Court 1731
Court convened 14 March 1731 at Elk River, continued until 18 March. Following commissioners present: Col. Benjamin Pearce, Capt. Richard Thompson, Capt. Edward Jackson, Capt. Thomas Colvill, Capt. James Alex-

ander, Mr. William Rumsey, Mr. Henry Ward, Mr. John Copson. Also present: John Campbell, sheriff, and Stephen Knight, clerk.

f.175 (DSC02284)
===

Petition of Reverend Hugh Jones.* States that the road by his house intrudes on the glebe and makes his house very open to the public, exposing his family to "the troublesome company and insults of many drunken, swearing fellows and makes us unsafe in our beds, and gives opportunity for thievish negroes and ordinary people, who continually pass that way, to corrupt and hinder our servants, and to pilfer anything that is left out by night, nay even to break open doors that are locked." Asks for the road to be rerouted to its former course which will be no longer or more inconvenient for travelers. Granted.

Petition of John Williams. Petitioner owns a tract called Rycroft's Choice, the bounds of which are decayed. Requests a commission be formed to investigate and confirm the bounds. Court appoints Capt. Edward Jackson, Robert Storey, Capt. Jethro Browne and Joseph Young as commissioners.

f.176 (DSC02284)
===

Petition of John Campbell. Petitioner owns a 300-acre parcel of a tract called Dividing on south side of Elk River. The tract had been resurveyed for himself and John Veazey and investigated by a commission which was unable to identify the second bounder. States that there are some old inhabitants who can identify the bounder and requests that a commission be formed to investigate and confirm same. Court appoints Col. Benjamin Pearce, William Rumsey, John Baldwin and Alphonso Cosden as commissioners.

June Court 1732
Court convened 13 June 1732 at Elk River, continued until 18 June. Following commissioners present: Col. Benjamin Pearce, Mr. John Hamond, Capt. Edward Jackson, Capt. James Alexander, Mr. John Copson, Capt. Richard Thompson, Mr. Henry Ward, Capt. Thomas Colvill, Mr. William Rumsey. Also present: John Campbell, sheriff, and Stephen Knight, clerk.

f.177 (DSC02285)

===

Petition of Richard Molynoux and sundry inhabitants of John Gilpin's (?) Neck.* States that the horse path laid out by William Rumsey and Dr. Hugh Matthews as directed by the court goes through his property and was poorly chosen because it is hilly and goes through the head of a creek which is often impassable. A better path out of the same neck would be through the plantations of John Wright and George Scott. Requests court to clear a new horse path accordingly. Signed by Richard Molynoux, Walter Scott, Walter Scott, Jun., Charles Scott, George Scott, Evert Everson, Jun., John Wright, Stephen Knight. Petition granted, with petitioners to clear the road at their own charge.

Petition of Anna Margarette Vanderheyden. Petitioner owns a tract called High Park originally granted to Richard Hash for 200 acres. Petitioner states that the bounds are precarious and requests that a commission be formed to investigate and confirm the bounds. Court appoints Col. Benjamin Pearce, John Baldwin, Nicholas Ridgley and John Penington as commissioners.

f.178 (DSC02285)

===

Petition of Peter Picoo (Pecoo). Petitioner owns a parcel of a tract called Capt. John's Manor where one of the bound markers was destroyed by malicious persons. Requests a commission be formed to investigate and confirm the bounds. Court appoints Mr. Thomas Johnson, Edward Johnson, John Kinkey and Nicholas Hyland as commissioners.

Petition of William Watson. Petitioner owns a tract called Yorkshire, the bounds of which are decayed. Requests a commission be formed to investigate and confirm the bounds. Court appoints Capt. Edward Jackson, John Copson, Stephen Onion and John Hamond commissioners.

Petition of Thomas Price. Petitioner owns a tract called Horns on the south side of Capt. John's Creek, originally patented to John Colett and George Goldsmith for 150 acres, the bounds of which are decayed. Requests a commission be formed to investigate and confirm the bounds.

93

Court appoints William Rumsey, Nicholas Ridgley, Alphonso Cosden and John Veazey commissioners.

f.179 (DSC02286)

==
Petition of John Thompson, son and heir of John Thompson, deceased. Petitioner owns a tract called Dunbar on south side of Bohemia and part of another called Corobo (Corobough), the bounds of which are decayed. Requests a commission be formed to investigate and confirm the bounds. Court appoints William Rumsey, Nicholas Ridgley, John Veazey and Alphonso Cosden commissioners.

Court adjourned until next session.

f.180 (DSC02286) No content

f.181 (DSC02287)

==

December Court 1732
Court convened 14 December 1732 at Elk River, continued until 16 December. Following commissioners present: Col. Benjamin Pearce, Mr. William Rumsey, Capt. Edward Jackson, Mr. John Copson, Capt. Richard Thompson, Capt. James Alexander. Also present: John Campbell, sheriff, and Stephen Knight, clerk.

Petition of Mary Rogers, widow of Thomas Rogers, deceased.* States that Archibald Trumble had lived with her deceased husband for years and now continues living with her. He is blind for some three years and incapable of work. Requests that he may be excused from the levy and asks for some allowance for supporting him. Court allows 150 lbs/tbco from present levy.

f.182 (DSC02287)

==
Petition of Joseph Moore.* States that a woman named Sarah Doore, sick with smallpox, had come to his house and stayed there eight or nine days before dying. She had no money or estate, and petitioner had to

cover all costs. States that he is himself very poor with a wife and four small children. Asks that court provide him with some allowance to help cover his costs. Court allows Moore 200 lbs/tbco for cost of Doore's burial.

Petition of Thomas and Richard Nash.* Petitioners state that they were bound as administrators of the estate of John Altham to his widow Mary Altham who has since remarried to "a certain Partitias Carol Carwen, a most extravagant man" who has been squandering the estate. Ask court to ensure proper redress is taken. Court orders that the estate be delivered immediately into the hands of the petitioners unless Carwen posts such security as the court approves.

f.183 (DSC02288)
==

Petition of Ann Beamont. Asks court for her annual salary for cleaning the courthouse and for continuation in their service. Court allows her 500 lbs/tbco.

Petition of John Baldwin. States that for past three years as sheriff he has not been allowed his 10 percent, as apparently was his due, on 24,200 pounds of tobacco of the levy because of omission. Asks court that provision be made in the current year's levy to pay him. Court directs that Baldwin be given 2,419 lbs/tbco from levy.

Petition of Gidion Pearce. States that he has been appointed by Kent County as keeper of the upper ferry for transportation "of man and horse" from Locust Point to Penington Point. Asks that he also be appointed as keeper of the upper ferry by Cecil County with appropriate compensation. Court agrees and allows Pearce 2,000 lbs/tbco for keeping the ferry for the year.

End of Court record. A brief and incomplete index appears on the final two folios of the original.

ADDENDUM

Petitions and Judgments, Cecil County Court, 1717-1732
Selected Transcriptions

f.0 (DSC02169) Court convenes March 1722.*
At a Court held at the Court house upon Sassafras
for Cecil County before his Lordships ----
thereunto authorized and appointed ----
tenth day of March Anno Dom. 1722
Comn'rs   Matthias VanBebber   John Jewart
Present   Francis Mauldin   Gunning Bedford

f.1 (DSC02169) Petition of James Gallaway concerning bastard children of Mary Emerson.
To the Worshipfull justices of Cecil County now sitting ----
The humble petition of James Gallaway sheweth that your
petitoner having been att Sundry Charges and trouble----
A Certain Mary Emerson servant of your said pet'nr who has
been lately delivered of two base born children by which your

pet'n hath Received damage and desireth that your worships----*
would take it into Consideration as usuall for the scandal to
his house etc.   Your petitioner as in duty bound shall pray
                              James Gallaway
Which petition being read and maturely considered ordered it is by the
Court that the sd Mary Emerson serves the said James nine months
over and above her indentured or covenanted term and
after the said nine months she be delivered up unto this Court
----to discharge trouble and disgrace of said Gallaways

f.4 (DSC02171) Petition of Mary Otheson for right to purchase old courthouse and lands.
To the worsipfull justices of Cecil County judicially sitting
The humble petition of Mary Otheson of sd County humbly sheweth
that whereas the County Court is now removed from Sasafrass river and
the old Court house and land thereunto belonging is of noe further

use or service to the Said County and understanding that your Worships are willing to dispose of the same your pet. humbly prays she may have the right of the sale or refusall thereof and your pet. as in Duty bound shall pray

Which petition being read and heard and maturely considered ordered it is by this Court that the same be granted-

f.6 (DSC02172) Petition of several inhabitants of Susquehanna Hundred to lay out a road.

To the right Worshipfull the Court of Quarter Sessions for Cecil County the humble petition of some of the inhabitants of Susquehana hundred sheweth That your petitioners being settled in a remote parte of of this country are destitute
of a convenient Road both to Church and Court also for rowling tobacco to a convenient landing and therefore humbly address themselves to the Court and humble request that it would please your Worships to grant an Order of Court for a Road to be laid out from the said Susquehana River to a plantation made by Roger Kerk being very convenient for the subscribers being your humble petitioners and your petitioners in duty bound shall pray for you –
--- Patton, Sam'l Brice, Enoch Enochson, Jonathan Johnes, Samuel Bowen, John Noland, Evan Brown, John Darlington, James Morriss, Jonas Mooun, Nath Barker, Henry Bowen, James Allmond, Roger Kerk, Barnat Rosenbein(?) Samuell Harris, William Lee, James Bond Robert Hand, --- Benett

Which petition being read and heard and duly considered by this Court the same is rejected.

f.6 (DSC02172) Petition of Ebenezer Cook to be admitted as attorney of court.

To the worshipfull the Justices of said County
The humble petition of Ebenezer Cook
sheweth that your petitioner having been a practitioner
in several courts of this Province prays leave
to be admitted in this Court in the same quality,
and your petitioner shall ever acknowledge the favor &c

The which petition being read and heard and duly considered
by this Court the same is granted he qualifying himself
according to Law, which he doth.

f.7 (DSC02172) Petition of William Jones to build public house next to courthouse.

The humble petition of William Jones sheweth
that your pet. having a licence to keep an ordinary in this County at
his dwelling plantation but it being remote from the Court house
desires leave of your Worships to suffer him to build a house upon the
Court house landing which God willing he intends convenient & useful for
entertaining your Worships and severall sutors to this court-
& your pet. shall ever pray &c   William Jones

Which petition being read & heard and duely considered by
this Court the same was granted, he complying with the laws in such
cases made & provided -

f.8 (DSC02173) Petition of Roger Larramore to have servant excused from county levy.

To the Worshipful justices of Cecill County now sitting –
The petition of Roger Laramore of sd County humbly sheweth that he hath
an oldnegro woman which is both lame and blind and wholly unable of
maintaining herself ofdoing anything toward her liveing for which reason
your petitioner desires that your Worships may please to allow her to be
free from paying levy & your petitioner as in duty bound will pray

Which petition being read and heard and duly considered by this Court it
is ordered that the same be granted.

f.9 (DSC02173) Record of sale of old Courthouse at Sassafras.

Ordered it is by this Court that the following persons three of his
Lordships Justices of the Peace viz. Mr. Mathias Bebber, Coll. John Ward
John Jawert, Commissioners thereunto especially appointed meet att the
old Courthouse on Sassafras River the 9th day of February next then &
there to hold Court to sell and dispose of the Old Court house att which
time & place the aforesaid Commissioners, Mr. Mathias Bebber, Coll.

John Ward and Mr. John Jawert meet to sell and dispose of the above named Court house with land belonging to the same for which thereof timely notice given for all persons to come in and bid for the same according to the following rules, viz. that the highest bidder should be the purchaserand that he shall be obliged to give securety & required to pay the sd bidas he offers to the Sheriff of said County next November Court, and that if any person bid he shall advance not less att a time than one hundred pounds of tobacco, the sdhouse and land to be putt up att two thousand pounds of tobacco. After a long deliberation and sundry persons bidd Coll. John Ward bidds and offers for the aforesd house and land five thousand seven hundred pounds of tobacco which being the highest offer the Court ordered that the said Coll. John Ward as being the highest bidd to have the said house and land belonging according for sd price –

f.10 (DSC02174)   Petition of Mary Hendrickham for support from her husband.

The humble Petition of Mary Hendrickham to the Worshipfull the Justices of this County humbly sheweth
(that) John Hendrickham my husband refuses to allow me any (support for) the maintenance of myself and child without any reason (given to) any person and to avoid any inconvenience or charge that may (come) through the inhumanity of my husband to the house inhabitants ---tey. Your petioner therfore prayeth that such methods may be taken for the securety of your petitioner and child that neither the petitioner nor child may be
subject to misery through the unlawfull and inhumane dealings of my husband in such way and manner as your worships shall think fit.
Your petitioner shall for ever as in duty bound pray &c

Mary Hendrickham

Which petition being read and heard ordered it is by the Court that summons issue Immediate for John Hendrickham that he be and appear att this Court to answer unto this complaint of the said Mary Hendrickham which accordingly isdone & he appears unto the same which petition haveing been read again therefore it is considered by this Court that the said John Hendrickham pay all fees due by his wife haveing being prosecuted on suspicion of bigamy-

f.11 (DSC02174) Petition of John Currer for relief from fine for nonappearance in jury.

To their Worships of Cecill County Court now sitting the humble petition of John Currer sheweth that whereas and by the order of Mr. Abell Burkeloo highSheriff of the County aforesd to Mr. Willian Dare his deputy sumoned your petitioner to appear as a jury man att this county court in August 1717, I and my family being then in good health was fully resolved to appear before your Worships
in the Court according to the tenour of the summons served on me
but some few days before the Court it pleased God to afflict my --
of mortall sickness insomuch that his sickness daly increased till the
day this Court began to sitt and upon that day about three a clock
it pleased god that he departed this life and that was the only cause (for me not to) appear according to the tenor of the summons which I can make --- if your worships are pleased to require it, and for my not appearing it was your Worships pleasure to fine me in the sum of five hundred pounds of tobacco. Your pet. humbly prayeth that you would be pleased to take off and remit Your pet. as is duty bound shall ever pray – John Currer

Which petition being read and heard and duely considered by this Court –
(No decision recorded.)

f.11 (DSC02174) Court convened 9 August 1720.

Att a Court held for Cecil County the 9th day of August 1720 at a Court house on Elk River before his Lordships justices thereunto authorized and appointed, viz.

Comr's Present	Mr. John Dowdall	Mr. Benjamin Pearce
	Mr. William Dare	Mr. Richard Thompson
	Mr. Roger Laramore	Mr. Edward Jackson

f.14 (DSC02176)   Petition of Elenor Collins on behalf of orphan being mistreated.

To the Worshipful the justices of Cecill County
The humble petition of Elenor Collins sheweth
That (nine?) years agoe a certain Thomas Heaptharpan orphan
in the care of your petitioner was by the then Justices of this Court bound

as an apprentice to a certain Thomas Rogers to learn the trade
of a tight cooper and the said Roger then alsoe obliged himself
to learn the said boy to write and read as by the records of
this Court may more fully appear – but the said Rogers contrary
to his agreement with their Worships hath not nor yett doth not
endeavour to instruct the said youth in the said trade or to write
or read but on the contrary compels the said youth to work
daily with the ax and hoe to the great damage of the said (youth)
and grief of your pet. and in contempt of your worships. (Your)
petitioner therefore humbly prays that your worships (will judge)
this matter and give such necessary orders concerning (the case)
as to your worships shall seem meett and your petitioner (&c)

Elenor Collins

Which petition being read and heard and duly considered by this Court
(it is) ordered by this Court that a summon be issued out agst Thomas
Rogersabovesaid (to) appear before this court and to bring the above
mentionedThomas Heaptharpan along with him
- and now the abovesaid Thomas Roger complying with said summons
and having the orphan boy along with him & this Court taking into their
due consideration the petition of the sd Elenor Collins ordered it is by this
Court that the sd petition be granted & that the sd boy be returned to the
care of the petitioner.

f.17 (DSC02177) Petition of Aron Latham to exchange building lot in Elkton.

To the worshipfull Justices of Cecill county –
The humble petition of Aron Latham sheweth –
that Mr. Jawart one of the members of this worshipfull (bench) having
pursuant to an order of this Court laid out severall lotts adjoyning to this
Court house to be built upon by such persons as should lawfully purchase
the same which purchasers were to have certificates of such lotts given
them by Mr. Jawart, and your petitioner having taken up three of the said
lotts on one of which your petitioner has built a small house, butt your
petitioner being determinedto build a large house fitt for the entertainment of travellers and othersand fearing to build upon either of his other
lotts which lye too near Wm.Jones House, least any accident of fire should
break out your petitionerwould willingly by your worships permission pur-

chase a lott nearer theriver side and quitt claim to his other two lotts not
built upon which yourpetitioner conceives may be the easier complyed
with since noebodyhas taken up these lotts upon the river nor any title
being madeto your petitioner for the other lotts. Your petitioner therefore
humbly prays that he may be allowed to build upon one of the said lotts
near the river and that your worships would be pleased to act such
necessary things in and about the premises for your petitioner's security
andyour petitioners title in and to the said lotts may be made good & val-
id --- your petitioner &c   Aron Latham

Which petition being read & heard and duly considered by this Court it is
ordered by the Court that the same be granted -

f.18 (DCS02178) Petition of the Inhabitants of New Munster objecting to changes being made to road.

To the right worshipfull his Lordships Justices on the
Bench at Cecil County Court house
humbly sheweth that we your petitioners look upon
you as gentlemen truly worthy of the honour wherewith
ye are dignifyed in having the trust and care of the good
order and well being of this County committed to your
charge we do with the more cheerfullness exhibit this
our petition to your worships. Some years since by the
clemency of this Court we obtained an order to make
a good sufficient road from the main road near
Thomas Jacobs to the outmost bound of New Munster
seven miles and more in length which was speedily done
with great labour and care to the great satisfaction
of our neighbours and strangers but now it seems we
are like to be deprived of the same through the undue
procurement of Lewis Jones and his complices who has
pretended to make a road & flop us out of---
as he exchanges for it is as followeth- First make ---
strike out to the left hand a great way down the river
where there is a steep bank and a deep and narrow
ford very dangerous which if we do escape we must
turn up the river a good way then down the river
again by a long and very high & dangerous bank

where there is no way to shun it and where hardly
any men on horse back will venture to ride much
less loaded horses or carts, when we have
escaped that danger it is as dangerous coming back
again. We humbly (pray) your worships will not expose us
and our posterity to such great difficulties & dangers &
that for no reason we know of unless it be to gratify the
covetous desires of a man who regards not the publick good
for if he pretends a damage for a road to go through
his land may not others pretend the same also as
well as he not doubting but that your worships
will do us justice we rest as in duty bound to pray
James Alexander, John Gillispe, Gavin Roper, David
Alexander, Arthur Alexander, John Wallas, James
McClure, James Alexander, Phillip Davis, Ely Alexander
Moses Alexander, William Pindergrass, Peter
Highgate, James Alexander.

Which petition being read and heard & duely considered
ordered it is by this Court here that the road stand as
it was formerly and be carefully cleared.

f.20 (DSC02179)   Petition of John Hollet to be appointed as guardian to son born out of wedlock.

To the worshipful Justices of Cecil County
The humble petition of John Hollet sheweth
that your petitioner is the reputative father
of a certain boy called John Hollet aged about
fourteen years the son of a certain Sarah Kerres
who in his infancy was bound by the Worshipfull the
then Justices of this County to a certain Paul Allen who
together with his wife is since dead (and) since whose death your
petitioners said reputed son is detained in the service of a certain James
Collins without any legall authority or consent of your petitioner.
Your pet. therefore humbly prays that as your pet. has been
at a great charge in maintaining the said boy and that
nobody has a more visible right for him than your petitioner that he
may be bound to serve your petitioner until he shall arrive at the

age of twenty one, and your petitioner etc -- John Hollett

Which petition being read and heard and duly considered by this Court it is ordered by the Justices that the same be granted and that the boy be delivered to the said Hollett.

f.22 (DSC02180) Petition of Clement Barkston for payment and renewal as keeper of Bohemia ferry.

To the worshipfull Justices of the peace for Cecil County in Court sitting the petition of Clement Barkston humble representeth that whereas your Worships were pleased to grant me your petitioner five thousand pounds of tobacco for keeping Bohemia Ferry the year last past I humbly request an order for the said wages and that you will permitt me to keep the said Ferry the year next ensuing. I submissively offer to your Worships that for whoever keeps this ferry this next year must pay four pounds currant silver money of Maryland to my Lord Baltimore & his agent for which reason I hope you will add equivalent to the wages it being some trouble to keep it as before and not soe great a draw back out of it. I leave it to your worships more mature consideration and relying on your candour in the same I subscribe myself your humble supplicant –
& shall ever pray &c   C. Barkston

Which petition being read & duly considered ordered it is by this Court Ordered that the same be granted he having the usuall allowance in that case made & provided.

f.24 (DSC02181) Petition of John Ham that his orphan godson be re-moved from Roman Catholic upbringing.

To the worshipfull the justices of Cecill County att Court judicially sitting the humble petition of John Ham sheweth –
that whereas your petitioner sometime agoe did stand godfather for a child of Edward Lewis of the afsd county named Evan Lewis and according to the custom of the Church of England then and there promised and engaged severall things in behalfs of the said child and whereas the afd Edward Lewis father of the said Even Lewis is since dec'd and the said Even now kept among Roman Catholicks contrary to the intention of his

105

Baptism your petitioner therefore humbly desires your worships that you would be pleasedto remove the said child to some other persons where he may be broughtup in the Church of England religious according to his baptism & your petitioner
shall pray -   John Ham

Which petition being read and heard and duly considered ordered it is by this court that the same be granted & said that Mary Lewis wife of the said Edward Lewis dec'd bring her son in law Evan Lewis to this court –

f.25 (DSC02181) Petition of Henry Hendrickson for reimbursement of charitable expenses.
Read the petition of Henry Hendrickson viz.
To the worshipfull the Justices for Cecill County
The humble petition of Henry Hendrickson sheweth –
that a certain Cane Allen (who in his life time) was a pensioner to this County became soe disabled in his limbs that he made application to your petitioner as overseer of the poor for crutches which your petitioner supplied him with as alsoe att his deathmake him a coffin to be buryed in therefore your petitioner hope your worships will allow him for the same –
     Crutches - - - 030
     Coffin - - - - - 200 lb tob
           230 –
No decision of the Court recorded.

f.25 (DSC92181) Petition of citizens to have Elk River ferry keeper replaced.
Read the petition of some of the inhabitants of Cecill County viz.
To the worshipfull justices of Cecill County sitting att a court to be holden for the said county att a court house upon Elk River Nov. 14th 1721
The humble petition of the subscribers inhabitants of said County in behalf of themselves & their neighbours most humbly sheweth – that whereas the County ferry over Elk River to and from our said Court house hath of late been kept by Negroes whose master being for the most part absent hath been very negligent in discharging their duty in keeping the said ferry to the great prejudice and disapointment of many &c   And for as much as your pet'nrs haveing conceived the afsd inconveniences as alsoe that the said ferry road hath proved very prejudicall to HermanKinkey

of the said county by cutting his land in severall parts soe as to renderit
inconvenient for cultivation whereby he may reasonably maintain his fam-
ily thereby all which your petitioner haveing duely considered as well in
the behalf of themselves as alsoe the prejudice and damage of the said
Kinkey and to remove the said prejudice damages inconveniences & dis-
apointment which hath and may accrew by the keeping the said ferry doe
therefore most humbly pray your Worships that the said Herman Kinkey
may have the priviledge of keeping the said ferry and enjoying the bene-
fitts thereof and your pet'nrs shall as bound in duty pray &
Robert Dutton, Thomas Hichcock, Alsaander Meceny, Ralph Rutter,
Gunning Bedford, William Currer, Darby Wheeling, Joseph Hollingsworth,
Henry Penington,Peter Mannadow, Richard Forster, William Howell, Hen-
ry Starr, John   Carsy, Evan---, Morgan Patten, David Wallace, Lewis Grif-
fith, John Bower, John Thomas, John Sim---, Richard Dobson, William and
Francis Jenkins, John Underhill, John Corer, Joseph Young, James Allmond,
William Corer, Ralph Barie, Johana Humberson,
Daniell Hukill, John Gray, William Husband, Gabriell Clement, John Ha---
William Sinclair, Henry Pennington, John Roberts, Math Matherson,
James H---, Roberd Dullon, Thomas Hichcock, James Allexander, Benjamin
Cox. Thomas Peirce, William Forster, John Court, Thomas Johnson, John
Sartill, Isaack Horssey,

Which petition being read and heard and duly considered by this court
ordered it is that the same be ~~granted~~ *rejected –*

f.26 (DSC92182) Petition for two bridges at heads of Elk River.

To the honourable justices for Ceecill county now holding Court for said
CountyThe humble petition of severall of the inhabittants of the said coun-
ty in behalf of themselves neighbours and strangers humbly sheweth that
whereas the great and main Kings Road leading through this his Lordships
Province of Maryland passing over the dangerous and swelling falls of the
twoheads of Elk River whereby many good people both inhabittants of
thisCounty as strangers are not only stopt and often disapointed in their
journeys to their loss and damage but likewise often in danger and perill
oftheir lives wherefore your petitioner humbly prays that the said hard-
ships inconveniency and damages might be prevented by ordering good
sufficient horse and foot bridges to be built over the said falls of the said

two heads of Elk River att the publick charges of the said County and your pet'nrs shall as in duty bound ever pray

Roger Merick, Richard Rutter, Thomas Beettle, Robert Eyre, Henry Reynolds, John Smith, Gavin Hutcheson, R Thatcher, R Dobson, William Forster, Hugh Lawson, David Rece, John Jones, Thomas Jacob, Henry Hollingsworth, Rowland Chambers, JosephHollingsworth, Adam Hollingsworth, Reneece Vancole, George Robinson, Zebulon Hollingsworth, John Thomas, Isaiah Phipps, Martin Cartmell, Stephen Hollingsworth,Martin Alexander, William Bristow, Richard Fredey.

Which petition being read & duly considered by this Court ordered it is that the same be rejected.

f.27 (DSC92182) Petition of William Carper to be released from indenture agreement.

To the worshipfull the Justices of Cecill County now sitting –

The humble petition of William Carper sheweth that your petitioner was a servant of a certain William Price of this County whom he honestly served the term of his sixyears and nine months – that during his abode with his said master and beforethe time of his servitude was expired your petitioner contracted with his said masterto give him his said master the funds of twenty shill(ings) for soe much of your peit'rstime of servitude as was then to come and be complied with which was threemonths ten shill^s of which twenty shill^s was to be paid att a certain day upon receipt of which ten shill the said William Price was to give your petitioner full discharge agst his indenture. That your pet'r on the his day appointed paid his said master the said ten shill which his said master accepted but refused to give your petitioner a discharge according to his promise and agreement. That your petitioner left said master with his consent but since hath caused your petitioner to be apprehended as a runaway & sold him to a certain John Veazey and with threats and malace frightened your petitioner to sign an indenture to serve the said Veazey for the space of two years – Your pet'r therefore humbly prays to be relieved in the premises & your pet'r shall ever pray ~~   William Carper

Which petition, being read & maturely considered ordered it is by this Court that the said William Carper serve his master John Veazey according to indenture &c.

108

f.27 (DSC92182) Petition for Cecil County to indict Sheriff James VanBebber for embezzling levy.

November the 14th 1721

To the worshipfull Justices of the said County

now in Court judiciously sitting the humble petition of the inhabitants & free holders of the aforesaid county sheweth that whereas James Van Bebber, Gent. late sherife of the aforesaid County on the twelfth day of Marchin the year one thousand seven hundred & nineteen did exact , levey and unlawfully take from the inhabitants of the aforesaid County the sum of eight thousand six hundred & one pounds of tobacco – which doth appear by a bill of inditement found against him the said James Van. Bebber by the Grand Jury of the said county; & that under some colour of friendship, relation, or otherwise the said inditement, is stifled & lies without bringing the said James Van Bebber to punishment as the law directs. Therefore we the subscribers being freeholders in the aforesaid county humbly pray, that since the Gent. that was commissioned at that time to prosecute his Lordships pleas – and dispense with his oath to that degree, wee the subscribers do pray that the said James Van Bebber may be brought before your worships & cause the aforesaid eight thousand six hundred & one pounds of tobacco to be returned in the laying of the levey that it may return to the persons from whom he unlawfully & unjustly took it. And your petitioners will as in duty bound ever pray   &c

James Allexander, Evan Reece, John Ward, A Burkeloo,
James Creagar, John Roberts, Hugh Matthews, Richard Thompson,
James Husbands, William Chick. Ephr. Aug. Herman, George Douglas,
Matt Matthiason, John Smith, John Hollett, William Veasey
William Husbands, Benjamin Cox, Robert Penington, Thomas Pearce,
William Price Jun., Henry Penington, Robert Dobson, John Dowdall,
Thomas Marcer, John Ham, John Thomas, Henry Ward,
John Numbers, Henry Penington Jun., Joseph Hollingsworth,
William Penington, John Campbell, Nicholas Dorrele, Allexander Macay,
Albert Cox, John Simonds, Aaron Lattham, Thomas Pope,
William Bristow, Thomas Johnson, Peter Picott, James Veasey,
John Marly, Joseph Lillifre, Richard Whitton, Walter Scott,
Robert Hodgson, Daniel Huikele, Cornelius Eliason, Henry Hendrickson,
Francis Steel, Thomas Croger &c –

Which petition being read wasby the Court postponed
for an hour and being read again James
Van Bebber comes into Court and promises to pay the County
the sum of tobacco mentioned in the said petition and the Court
orders the same to be inserted in this present Levy –

f.29 (DSC02183) Petition of Joshua George to be admitted as attorney.

To the worshipfull the justices of Cecil County court.
the humble petition of Joshua George sheweth –
That your petitioner has had the favour of being admitted
a practitioner into the Chancery and Prov. Courts and severall other courts
in this Province and humbly prays your Worships to be admitted as
an attorney of this Court, and your petitioner shall pray &c

Joshua George

The which petition being read, heard and maturely considered ordered
it is by this Court that the same be granted he the said Joshua
George qualifying himself according to law & whereupon the
said Joshua takes the attorneys oath & other usuall oaths appointed
signing the Ooath of Abjuration & the text &c according to Law.

f.29 (DSC02183) Petition regarding encroachment of Chester County surveyor into Cecil.

To the worshipfull Justices of Cecill County at a Court held
for the said county that second Tuesday of June instant,
The humble petition of Samuell Brice of the said county
most humbly sheweththat whereas your petitioner have been an
inhabitant of this county on New Conough Mannor for about nine
years past, & have always quietly & peaceably paid all taxes
and duty to this county since an inhabitant, within the jurisdiction
of this Court &c. Butt so it is may it please your Worships that about
the 11the of this instant, the surveyor for the county of Chester of the
Province of Pensillvania with others assisting him came and
surveyed close to your petitioners fence soe as to render your
petitioners settlement altogether inconvenient for the use of
your petitioner & greatly to his prejudice/and further that
your petitioner is very credibly informed that Daniell Smith,

George Sluytor, James Bond, John Bond, Edward Long, John Allen,
Charles Allen, and severall others are upon complying with a
Pensilvania survey and title, altho they have considerable
time since complyed with and allowed themselves inhabitants
of this County all which your petitioner conceives in not only
an agreivance to your petitioner, but to the public interest
of this Government and his Lordships good rule & loudly calls
for redress, and for which your petitioner prays &c
Samuel Brice

The which petition being read and by the Court heard and
maturely and deliberately considered, ordered it is that a
precept be made out, imediately and from this Court directed to
the Sheriff of Cecill county to take and bring the body of Isaac
Taylor serveyor of Chester County aforesaid and all other persons
concerned in the breach of the peace in the said petition
mentioned by reason of their surveying as aforesaid to answer
to this Court concerning the said breach. Which precept was
accordingly issued.

f.30 (DSC02184) Petition of Elizabeth Sluyter to choose her guardian.
To the worshipfull the justices of Ceecill County in court
judicially sitting the humble petition of Elizabeth Sluyter
sheweth. That whereas your petitioners father is lately
deceased, and your petitioner being at age to choose guardians
humbly prays that your worships may appoint your petitioners
brother Benjamin Sluyter her guardian and your petitioner
shall pray &c –   *Elizabeth Sluyter*
June the 13ᵗʰ 1722.

The which petition being read, & heard was bythe Court considered and
granted &c.

f.31 (DSC02184) Petition of William Bristow for assistance on medical
costs for his orphaned godson.
To the worshipfull the justices of Cecill County now sitting
the petition of William Bristow in the behalf of a godson of
his and only son of Edward Luis of the said county deceased

humbly sheweth that whereas one Edward Luis of this county
deceased has left his son with a gracious sore legg
and no affects or anything vissabell for the boys cure or sustenance
whereof the lad has made his address to your petitioner being
his godfather and I in his behalf to your worships as being the
father of the orphans, therefore your petitioner craved that,
your Worships will consider the languishing condition that the
boy is left in, and take in into your tender fatherly care that,
the boy may have some cure and mainainance and your
petitioner shall as in duty bound ever pray &c   William Bristow

The which petition being read, heard & maturely considered
ordered it is by this Court that the said William Bristow take
care that a cure be performed upon the orphan boy mentioned
in his said petition, and that he shall be allowed by this
Court all reasonable charges towards the same at next
November Court

f.32 (DSC02185) Petition of William Sinclear to be appointed guardian of orphan.

To the worshpfull Justices of Cecill County in Court
judicially sitting the humble petition of William Sinclear
sheweth – that whereas your petitioner hath his six years
past & better carefully brought up and maintained a certain
George Lancaster an orphan of this county (being your pet'rs
sisters son) and hath given the said orphan some school
and is willing to continue the same case, but the said
orphan now being at the age of fourteen years & at
capacity to choose guardians; it is humbly prayed that
your Worships may take the matter in your care so
far as to appoint him some carefull guardians (either
your petitioner or else whome your Worships shall think
fitt and your petitioner shall pray &c   William Sinclear

The which petition being read heard & considered by this
Court it is granted & ordered & appointed that your petitioner
William Sinclear be guardian to the orphan menconed
in the said petition

f.34 (DSC02186) Petition of Jacob Archer to levy damages on his runaway servant.

*Jacob Archer proves an account about his servant Hugh Morris's run
away time being 11 days, likewise for expences in taking him up
£2:10:8 and ordered it is by this Court that the aforesaid Hugh Morris
serve his said master over and above his indentured time of
servitude 200 days besides the runaway time formerly adjudged.*

f.34 (DSC02186) Petition of Robert Willson to be released from imprisonment as suspected runaway.

*The humble petition of Robert Willson sheweth
that the petitioner some time ago was committed by
M. Matthias Van Bebber to the common prison of this county on
suspicion of being a runaway, where your petitioner has quietly
remained and no person made the least claim of your petitioner
or charged him with any crime whatsoever. Your petitioner
therefore humbly prays your worships judgment that he your
petitioner may be discharged from the Sheriffs custody &c and
your petitioner &c ~~~*   *Robert Willson*

*The which petition being read heard and by the Court duly considered
ordered it is per curia that the same be granted and the petitioner
discharged*

f.36 (DSC02187) Petition of Bartholemew Johnson for reimbursement of charitable expenses.

*To the worshipfull Justices of Cecil County.
The humble petition of Bartholomew Johnson of the
said County most humbly shewth
that a certain traveller was found on the main road
speechless by Adam Wallace and your petitioners wife, near
your petitioners house, by which means as bound in Christian
duty your petitioners wife and the said Adam Wallace brought the
said traveller to your petitioners house, where after some time,
he there dyed, whome your petitioner buryed in as decent a
manner as his circumstances would allow and for that the
said traveller was a stranger and being speechless could never*

understand his circumstances or place of abode, & having
nothing about him to satisfy your petitioner for his charges
& troubles, and your petitioners circumstances being such that
he cannot afford the said trouble service & charges for nothing
except to the prejudice of his family, having many small children
Therefore humbly prays of your worships a reasonable
allowance from the publick to the said expences and trouble
and your petitioner shall pray &c   Bartholomew Johnson

The which petition being heard & maturely considered, ordered
it is by the justices held in court this day aforesaid that the said
petitioner be allowed four hundred pounds of tobacco in
this present levy

f.39 (DSC02188) Petition of William Howell, clerk of North Elk Parish, for funds for church expenses.

To the worshipfull the Justices of Cecil County in Court sitting
the humble petition of the vestry of North Elk humbly sheweth
that whereas your petitioners having an occasion of tobacco to ---
for the church at the said parish and to repair sundry things relating
to the church, humbly pray that your worships would assess in the
publick levy as the Act of Assembly in such case made & provided
shall allow and your petitioners shall pray &c
                    Signed per ord: of the Vestry
                    William Hollingsworth

The which petition being read, heard and maturely considered by the Justices the same is granted, and the said parish ordered to be assessed ten
pounds of tobacco p/ pole in the present levy for the use of the said
Parish church &c-

f.40 (DSC02189) Petition of John Thomas concerning cost overages in building bridges at head of Elk.

To the worshipfull Justices of Cecil County judicially sitting.
The humble petition of John Thomas most humbly sheweth
that whereas your petitioner agreed with your Worships
for the building two bridges over the two branches of Elk River
which your petitioner have performed, but so it is may it

please your worships that your petitioner not well considering
the value of the building the said bridges, at the time of agreeing
for the building the same, finds a great deal more
work that your petitioner expected – for which your petitioner
humbly prays your worships that you would please to order
two discreett persons to view the said bridges & make
report of the same to this worshipfull court of the value of
building the said bridges, and your petitioner is willing to
be content with such as by those persons shall be adjudged
the value of building the same, & your petitioner shall pray
November the 16th: 1722 -   *John Thomas*

The which petition being read, heard, and maturely
considered by the justices here in court ordered it is that
John Thomas the petitioner be allowed according to former
agreement with him the sum of seven thousand pounds of
tobacco in this present levy for the building of said bridges

f.41 (DSC02189) Memorandum concerning replacement of ferrymen.
Memmourandom. It is mutually agreed by the Justices
afsd, as a standing rule of this Court that in case any just complaint be
made, against the ferry men of this County, before two Justices of the
peace
that then it shall be in their power to turn out such delinquant and
put in another in his stead and place.

f.42 (DSC02190) Petition of Barnard Brock to be made tax free.
To the right honourable & worshpfull his Lordships Justices of
the hounourable bench assembled in Court for the County of Cecil –
The humble petition of Barnard Brock a resident within this
County of Cecill sheweth whereas your humble petitioner having
through much difficulty endeavoured hitherto to answer & have paid
the levys due from me upon the publick account of the County, and
through an accident which lately happened, one of my arms is
broken, & now lye in a deplorable condition, not able to help myself
but lye upon expenses endeavouring to gett help, which cure
cannot be soon expected if ever, by reason of age and feebleness which
hath this many years afflicted me sorely. Now I your petitioner

desire that this my tax or levy may be remitted, as likewise hereafter for the abovesaid reasons that I may no more be listed as a
taxable in the Constables list. And your petitioner as in duty bound
shall ever pray ~~   Barnard Brock
Wee whose names are here under written do signifie that the abovesaid
petitioner hath been an honest, laborious, & charitable man as far as in
him lay and he hath been feeble in his limbs this many years scarce able to
make a livelihood ~~ We knowing his condition do desire and request that
he no more may be accountable for paying tax hereafter r ~~~ & so wee
rest your humble servants to command
                                    Evan Jones .   Stephen Ross
                                    Isaac James   Hugh Ross
                                    Thomas Cochran
The which petition being read, heard, and by Justices here in Court duly
and charitably considered ordered it is that the same be granted and the
petitioner allowed two hundred pounds of tobacco in this present levy to
pay his tax &c ~~~

f.43 (DSC02190) Petition of Gunning Bradford for expenses accrued in hosting governor and council.

To the worshpfull the Justices of Cecil County ~
May it please your Worships you may remember that the
past November court I delivered in my account for the Governour
and the Councils expenses at my house amounting to fourteen
pounds two shillings and two pence and the Court was then
pleased to allow of it, and was entered on the file accordingly;
but afterwards ordered to be razed of the file again very much
to my loss and detriment, hope's your worships will now lett
me have credit for it this levy and I shall be in duty bound &c
                                    Gunning Bedford
The which petition being read and heard, was by the
Court granted as per note filed by the Committees for
laying or settling the levey's

f.44 (DSC02191) 12 Court convened March 1722.

At a Court held for Cecil County at the Court house
upon the Elk River the second Tuesday in March the
twelfth day , continued the thirteenth, fourteenth, fifteenth,

and sixteenth days of said month in the eigth year of the
Dominion of Charles Absolute Lord and Proprietary of the
Province of Maryland and Avalon, Lord Barron of
Baltimore &c Anno Dom. 1722 by his Lordships
Justices and Officers thereunto appointed and
authorized of whome were   The Worshipfull

Commr's	*Mr. Matthias Van Bebber*	*Mr. Samuel Alexander*
Present	*Col. Benjamin Pearce*	*Mr. Stephen Hollingsworth*
	Mr. Edward Jackson	*Mr. James Alexander*
	John Hack, Sheriff	*Stephen Knight, Clerk*

Mr. Francis Mauldin, one of the Justices mentioned in the Commission of
Oyer & Terminer bearing date the 3rd Nov'br 1722 takes the usual
Oaths & subscribes to the Oath of Abjuration & the Test & takes
His seat upon the bench ~~~   Mr. Henry Ward sitts
Then the Court adjourned till tomorrow morn 8 a clock.

f.45 (DSC02191) Petition of Joseph Wood for clearing a road from Back Creek towards New Castle.

The petition of Joseph Wood humbly sheweth that
whereas there was a road laid out by the order of Court
formerly over the head of Back Creek and so on to the road
that goes to New Castle which said road never was
cleared & tis very dangerous for travellers to ride on
the same, so your petitioner humbly prayeth the
honourable bench, to appoint men to oversee the
same & that it be well cleared & your petitioner shall
always pray as in duty bound ~~~   Joseph Wood

The which petition being read heard and duly considered
by the Justices aforesaid here in our said court the same
is granted & ordered that a clause be inserted in the overseer's
warrant of that hundred to clear the said road as far
towards New Castle as where the Pensilvanians leave
off, and the petitioner Joseph Wood appointed
inspector to see the same well cleared

f.47 (DSC20192) Petition of Joseph Burchmore for release from fraudulent indenture.

To the worshipfull the justices of Cecill County
The humble petition of Joseph Burchmore sheweth
that your petitioner in unjustly detained as a
servant by a certaine John Kimber of this county under pretence
of having an indenture signed by your petitioner to the said Kimber
which indenture was surreptitiously obtained by the said
Kimber from your petitioner& your petitioner therefore humbly
prays your worships releife in the premises etc.
Your petitioner shall ever pray ~ Joseph Burchmore

The which petition being read heard & duly considered---
by the Justices aforesaid here in Court, it is by them adjudged
and ordered that the said John Kimber former master of
petitioner shall with all convenient speed provide & give
him the said petitioner his freedom dues according to Law
and that for his time of over servitude which he hath been
detained since he justly ought to have been free he now
give him four hundred pounds of tobacco

f.48 (DSC02193) Petition for laying of road from Elkton to Christiana and New Castle.

To the worshipfull the Justices of Cecill County sitting
The petition of the upper inhabitants of Cecil County humbly
Sheweth that whereas your petitioners to the great inconveniency
both of themselves and travellers have no roads from
the foard at the head of Elk River to New Castle, nor to Christeen
Bridge, the former road not being layd out by order of
Court, that it is soe stoped and turned that carts is forced to go
by New Munster Road tho' a long way further, and strangers
& travellers go oft down to French Town instead of the head of
Elk River. The Welsh having cleared and marked a road that —
Strangers can find as far as their supposed bounds and from
whence we have no marked road that strangers can find,
wherefore your petitioners humbly pray that your worships
would be pleased to grant an order for a road from the said head
of Elk River till it entersects the road from New Castle and

another while it entersects the road from Christeen Bridge &
to order or appoint two men to lay out the same & in duty
bound your petitioners shall ever pray &c ~~~

Gunning Bedford	John Buchanan	William Bristow
Thomas Russell	Adam Wallace	Bartill Johnson
Stephen Onion	James Wallace	Peter Barker
John Hack	Marlin Alexander	William Thomas
--- Hollingsworth	Francis Alexander	Henry Runalls
--mon Johnson	Richard Dobson	Thomas Jacobs
--- Hendrickson		

The which petition being read heard and by the court duly considered
the same was granted & ordered it was by the justices of
that William Bristow overseer of Bohemia hundred and
Thomas Jacobs wee the said roads mentioned in the said
petition laid out and made

f.49 (DSC02193 Petition of Inhabitants of Milford Hundred for laying road to Hollingsworth's mill.

To the worshipfull Justices of Cecil County judicially sitting
The humble petition of severall of the inhabitants
of Milford Hundred most humbly sheweth
that whereas there is necessity of a road from the road
of New Munster at David Alexanders convenient across
Elk River main fresh to the Church Road at or near Mr.
Stephen Hollingsworths mill, which said road we the
subscribers humbly conceive will be of great service
both to the inhabitants and strangers travelling that way.
Therefore we the subscribers most humbly pray
an order from this worshipfull Court to erect & clear the said
road to & for the best conveniency for the nighest and best
travelling & maintaining the same, and we shall ever as

bounden in duty pray ~~	James Young	Alexander White
Martin Cartmill	Thomas Broun	John Segar
Jonathan Curtis	Joseph Teell	Tobias James
Joseph Hollingsworth	Thomas Sharp	George Robinson
Richard Cleyton	James Andrews	Robert Holey
John Finlow	Phillip Davis	James Mafat

The which petition being read heard and maturely considered the
same was granted & ordered it was by the Justices afsd
here in court the day and year aforesaid that Jonathan Curtis and
Martin Cartmill be inspectors to see the road prayed for
In said petition laid out and well cleared.

f.50 (DSC02194) Petition of Stephen Onion concerning indenture of Mary Seale and her children.
The petition of Stephen Onion of the aforesaid county
humbly sheweth that your petitioner having
sent to him by partners in England several indented servants
viz. one Matthias Seale his wife and five children, the said
Matthias dying in nine months after his arrival. The wife &
children since his death conceive the indenture made by
the said Matthias Seale void or of little & no force, the wife &
children having not sealed & signed the same, though bound by
her husband & their father, and have and do neglect your
petitioners business, and refuse to obey his lawfull commands
to the great prejudice of his selfe and partners –
Your petitioner therefore humbly prayeth that summons
may issue forth from this worshipfull court to bring Mary
Seale the aforesaid wife of the late Matthias Seale, & Matthias
Joseph, Samuell, James & Mary their children, to answer to
the complainant and that the said parties may either by said
indenture or by the customs of the country be obliged to serve
your petitioner and your petitioner shall pray.

Stephen Onion

The which petition being read and together with the alligations
of the complainant and defendant heard and maturely and
deliberately considered it was by the Justices aforesaid here in afsd
Court adjudged that the said Mary Seale & her children
could not be held as servants by the said indenture or other
wise as in the said petition set forth and ordered it was
that Mr. Stephen Onion the aforesaid complainant take into his
care and charge the five children of said Mary Seale by name

120

mentioned in his petition and to bring them here at next
August court

f.51 (DSC02194) Petition of John Hinkley to have his indenture terminated and freedom dues paid.

The humble petition of John Hinkley to the
worshpfull the Justices of Cecil County sheweth
that your petitioner hath legally and honestly served a
certain Peter Carmicke of this county, Gent, for & during the full
term & space of four years. Nevertheless the said Peter refuseth
to discharge your petitioner or to pay him the freedom dues of this
Province as by the laws of the said province allowed him.
Wherefore your petitioner humbly prays your Worships
order for his said freedom & dues and that he may have a
discharge from his said late master, and your petitioner
as in duty bound shall ever pray.   John Hinkley
Mr. Peter Carmicke appears to the said petition according
to summons, and in his defense objects that the said
John Hinkely did not faithfully serve him or labour in
his service on the twelfth day of Aprill last past.
Whereupon the said John Hinkley makes oath that on the
12th day of Aprill 1723 he the said deponent did do a days
work upon his master Peter Carmicke's plantation & in
service as a servant to his said master.
John Slider sworn evidence per Hinkley
Joanes Umbers summoned & sworn per ditto

And the court haveing fully heard all the alligations on each
side as well as the evidences and the petition upon a
mature and deliberate consideration of the premises ordered
it was by the Justices aforesaid that the said Peter
Carmicke within a convenient time provide & give his said
late servant John Hinkley his freedom dues according to
Act of Assembly

f.52 (DSC02195) Petition of Milford Hundred inhabitants for improvement of road.

To the worshpfull Justices of Cecil County judiciallysitting,

The humble petition of severall of the inhabitants
of Milford hundred most humbly sheweth ~~
That whereas there hath been a road laid out form the
branches of Elk river to the Church at North East & as may
appear, which upon experience proves difficult dangerous
and troublesome to maintain & by reason of crossing
severall branches particularly the east branch of North
East River twice with severall other small branches
that the same was granted but for a bridle road –
but for-as-much as daily experience sheweth that there
Is great necessity of a cart road to and from the said place
and alsoe that the said road might be layd out & cutt
a considerable deal nearer and on better ground avoiding
the severall branches and dangers before mentioned
to and for the great advantage conveniency and ease of
the inhabitants travellers and strangers –

Therefore wee the subscribers most humbly pray
a warrant & order to the Supervisor of the roads of the northwest
parts of Milford hundred or some other discreet person to
alter or now lay out the said road convenient etc to the best
advantage of travellers etc and to clear the same according
to law. And your petitioners shall as bound in duty pray.
Francis Wallace, Abraham Hollingsworth, Joseph Hollingsworth
John Spie, Alexander White, James MacClear, Walt Carr
Reneez VanCoolen, William Maffitt, Samuel Maffitt,
Samuel Bond, Tobias James, Matthew Hodgson, Hugh
Lawson, Jonathan Curtis, William Gorrell, Thomas Sharpe,
John Thomas, John Mare, Zebulon Hollingsworth,
Robert Holy, Martin Cartmill ~~~

The which petition being read heard & maturely
considered of, the same was granted, and ordered it was
by the Justices aforesaid, that M. Stephen Hollingsworth
should be inspector to see the said road menconed in the
said petition layd out, to see the same might be cleared,
not to demnifie any inhabitants of said hundred.

f.58 (DSC02198) Petition of Joanna Dampeir for charitable allowance.

To the worshpfull Justices of Cecill County now sitting
The petition of Joanna Dampeir humbly sheweth –
that whereas your petitioner being a poor widow & has
great charge of children and being so very lame that she is
not able to live any longer without some assistance ,your
petitioner having spent what little was left her by her husband
in bringing up her children and now your petitioner being advised
to apply herself to a doctor but being so very poor cannot
without your worships will be pleased to take pitty on her
wherefore your petitioner humbly prays an allowance of two
thousand pounds of tobacco & your petitioner shall pray.
    ~~~~~~~~~~   *Joanna Dampeir*
The which petition being read heard and maturely considered ordered
it is by the Justices afsd here in court the same day and year afsd
that the said Joanna Dampeir be allowed twelve hundred
pounds of tobacco in this leavy towards her maintainance.

f.63 (DSC02200) Petition of Sheriff John Hack for assistance in hanging convicted prisoner.

To the worshipfull the Justices of Cecil County
The humble petition of John Hack sheweth –
that your petitioner having in his custody a certain
Robert Dutch, who is condemned to be hanged the nineteenth
day of this instant June and your petitioner being fearfull
thro the insufficiency of a goal (jail) humbly requests
your worships order to provide a sufficient standing guard
in order to secure the said prisoner, till he is brought
to condign punishment and which your petitioner is
informed is usuall to be allowed to the Sheriff both
of this and the neighbouring government, as also for
an order to summon the Constables of the several hundreds
of the said County to be at your petitioners goal
at 8 a clock in the morning on the 19th day of this instant
June in order to be assisting in bringing the above
prisoner to the place of execution and your
petitioner will ever pray.   *John Hack Sheriff*

Which petition being duly considered it is
ordered by the Justices here in Court the same day and
year aforesaid that the Sheriff summons two men to
watch and ward the prisoner mentioned in the afsd
petition and that the said two men be allowed a satisfaction
for their trouble and expenses at the laying of
the next levey and that the Constables be summoned
to attend as prayed.

f.64 (DSC20201) Petition of Matthias Van Bebber to enforce indenture on recalcitrant servant.

To the worshipfull justices sitting in Court –
This is humbly to desire you to favour me to send
my servant Garret Bann for to have him judged
according to an Act of Assembly provideth for servants
come in without indenture & also to hear my further
complaints against him. I should not have troubled
your worships if I was able to bring him
but I do protest that I am not able to make him do
anything but what he pleases and without your
insistance shall be forced to set him free which
I hope you'l I prevent by administration of justice
As is humbly prayed by your most humble servant
                ~~~~~~~~~~~~ Mathias Ven Bebber

Which petition being duly considered by the Justices
aforesaid here in Court the day and year aforesaid
an order is by them given to Daniel Hakili Constable to bring
the body of Garret Bann to appear at this Court to answer
the complaint of his said master and the said Garret Benn
appearing according to sumons to answer the allegation
and complaint the Court adjudges that the said Garret
Bann serve his said master or his assigns five years
commencing from the time of the ships anchoring in Maryland
that brought the said Garret Bann in, which arrivall
was the 25th November 1722. Also the court orders that
the Sheriff take the said Garret Bann to the Whipping
Post and give him 25 lashes upon the bare back well laid on -

f.68 (DSC02203) Petition of Thomas Johnson concerning appointment as ranger of Cecil County.

To the worshipfull Justices of Cecil County
Judicially sitting prayeth –
That whereas the said county of Cecil is at present
without any ranger and your petitioner
being desirous to procure his excellences the present
Governours commission for the same
which your petitioner is not capable to obtain without
your worships recommendation your petitioner
therefore humbly prays your Worships to
(testifie) under your hands your petitioner to be a
(proper) person to be Ranger of the abovesaid County and
that your petitioner is also a person of good name fame
and repute, or such other recommendations as your
Worships shall think proper and your petitioner shall
ever pray   ~~~~~   Thomas Johnson

Which petition being duly considered the
Justices aforesaid proceed to give the petitioner
such recommendation as is required by Act
of Assembly

f.72 (DSC02205) Petition of James Andrews et al. for clearing of road providing access to mill.

To the worshipfull the Justices in Court now sitting
Your petitioners haveing lately built a mill upon a
branch of Elk River and their being no highway near
the said mill your petitioners humbly beg you will
grant an order to mark a way from the said mill to the
Kings highway that leads to Elk Landing and likewise
to the highway leading to North East or to other market places
and your petitioners will make the same ways not touching
any mans inclosures, upon our own charges and your
petitioners as in duty bound shall ever pray &c ~~~
James Andrews, James Hobetts, Roger Lawson, James Mathet,
John Hogsitt, Abram Hollingsworth, Morgan Pattan,

Thomas Sharp, Robert Holy.

The which petition being duly considered by the Justices
aforesaid here in Court the day and year aforesaid
the same is granted, the petitioners clearing the same roads
at their own charge. & that road which leads
to Chambers to go through his lane.

f.73 (DSC02205) Petition of Benjamin Allen for bounty on squirrel heads.

The humble petition of Benjamin Allen - your petitioner
humbly sheweth that whereas your petitioner last November
Court did send a note to the committey from under the hand of
Capt. Edward Jackson one of his Lordships Justices for the said
County for one wolfs head and thirty eight squirrills
heads and by some manner or other your petitioner never had
any credit given for them as above said wherefore your petitioner
humbly prays that you would allow him for them and your
petitioner as in duty bound shall pray. Benjamin Allen.

Which petition being duly considered by the Justices aforesaid
here in the day and year aforesaid the same is granted.

f.73 (DSC02205) Petition of Cornelius McCormack for bounty on squirrel heads.

To the worshipfull the Justices of Cecil County in Court
now sitting the humble petition of Cornelius McCarmack
humbly sheweth that whereas your petitioner last November Court did
bring into the comittey a note for eighty six squirrils heads & two
crows and by some mistake is allowed but two hundred & fifty
six pounds of tobacco less than is your petitioners due . Therefore
your humble petitioner humbly prays that he may have
the remainder allowed to him and as in duty bound shall pray
Cornelius MacCarmack.
The which petition being duly considered by the Justices
aforesaid it is ordered the petitioner have one hundred
pounds of tobacco this present levy.

f.75 (DSC02206) Petition of Jane Davis complaining of excessive debt recovery against her.

To the worshipfull Justices of Cecil County –
The humble petition of Jane Davis the wife of Frances
Davis of the said County humbly sheweth that whereas
your petitioners husband being from home and being
indebted to Hugh Mathews of the same County in the sum
of thirty shillings currant money (for) which the said Mathews
obtained an atachment for the goods of your petitioners
husbands which was all executed and carried from your
petitioner to her great disappointment being a far greater
(value than) the debt but so it is may it please your Worships
your petitioner carried wheat for the debt & cost to the
Sheriffs to discharge the said goods & debt which he
refused but would not let your petitioner have her goods
for which your petitioner prays your worships for an order
for her goods or that the Sherriff might show reasons to
your worships to the contrary & your petitioner shall
pray ~~~~   Jane Davis
The which petition being duly considered of by the
Justices aforesaid here in Court he day and year aforesaid
they give orders that the petitioner have her goods restored
to her again.

f.76 (DSC02207) Petition of Thomas Pimm for charitable allowance.
Read the petition of Thomas Pimm viz.
To the worshipfull Justices of Cecil County in Court judicially
sitting The humble petition of Thomas Pimn of Cecil
County sheweth that your petitioner has been an
inhabitant of this county for twelve years past or there about
and now being about seventy three years of age and
much afflicted with sickness and lameness is not able
for to labour for maintainance therefore humbly
prays that your worships would extend your charity towards
your poor petitioner and order him such allowance in
the publick as may be sufficient for him to subsist
on and your petitioner shall ever pray & etcetera.

The which petition being duly considered by the
Justices aforesaid here in Court the day and year afsd
It is ordered that the said Thomas Pimm be allocated as a poopr pensioner
the sum of four hundred pounds of tobacco in this present levy.

f.77 (DSC02207) Petition concerning possible blockage of roads in Susquehanna Hundred.

To the worshipfull the Justices of Cecil County now in
Court judicially sitting – the humble petition of your petitioner
humbly sheweth that whereas your petitioners having made a rowling
road for the conveniency of sundry of the inhabitants of Susquehannah
Hundred for the rolling of tobacco to Susquehannah: and since have
kept the road clear on their own charge: but since the said roads is in
some likelyhood to be stopt up to the damage of your petitioners
wherefore your petitioners humbly prays that your Worships would
be pleased to grant and order for the said roads and your petitioners
as in duty bound shall pray   Cornelius McCarmack, William
Curer, Samuel Buie, George Martain, Richard Abiall, John
Partill, John Longue - - - - ------

Which petition being duly considered by
theJustices aforesaid here in Court the day and year aforesaid it is
ordered that the roads mentioned in the petition be continued as it was
formerly cleared.

f.81 (DSC02209) Petition of Mary Parsons asking that two old slaves be made tax free.

To the worshipfull Justices of Cecil County in court sitting.
The humble petition of Mary Parsons administratrix of William
Parsons deceased humbly sheweth that your petitioner hath
two slaves belonging to the estate of your petitioners deceased
husband that is unable to earns their victualls by occasion of their
age being the one is eighty years old & the other above seventy
your petitioner humbly prays that your worships will grant
that the said two slaves may be levey free for the future and your
petitioner will as in duty bound ever pray.   Mary Parson.

The which petition being duly considered by the Justices aforesaid

here in Court the day & year aforesaid it is order'd by said Justices
that one of the Negroes mentin'd in the petition named Tom be
levey free.

f.83 (DSC02210) Petition of Joseph Young asking that ailing man in his care be made tax free.
To the worshpfull Justices of Cecil County now sitting.
The humble petition of Joseph Young most humbly sheweth
that whereas your petitioner had the care of one Benjamin Clark, a
native of this Province for whome he hath paid a levey yearly for
sundry years past imediately out of his own pocket, the said Benjamin
not being of a condition even to earn his own victualls by reason
of an incurable malady which hath afflicted him for some years
past, throwing him into convultion fitts sometimes fifteen or sixteen or
twenty times a week the verity of which is well known to the
neighborhood. Your petitioner therefore humbly prays that your petitioner
may be exempted from paying of leveys for the said Benjamin for the
future and your petitioner &c ~~~
-
Which petition being duly considered by the Justices aforesaid
here in Court the day & year aforesaid the said Justices order the said
Benjamin hereafter be levy free.

f.84 (DSC02211) Petition of Edward Smith to have kidnapped orphan returned to him.
To the worshipfull the justices of Cecil County Court.
The humble petition of Edward Smith of Baltimore County
sheweth unto your worships that about six years agoe
one William Burney then lately arrived from Ireland with a
large family of small children & settled in Baltimore County
nigh your petitioner & in short time the said Burney
& his family through long sickness were reduced to great want
insomuch that your petitioner for compassion to the said Burney
& his family took them into his Petitioners own house & took the best
care of them he could & continued so to do untill five of them
died, & the others recovered, which said five was buried decently
at the charge of your petitioner. Your peititoner further humbly
sheweth that the said Burney in his life time in his perfect

129

health as likewise on his death bed recomended & gave one of
his children named Thomas Burney then an infant of about
six years of age unto your petitioner until he should come to the
age of one and twenty years of whome your petitioner for almost
six years took good care of & used as his own child yet now so it
may it please your Worships that in June last your petitioner
mist the said Thomas Burney very sudenly to his great surprise
as well as of severall of his neighbours which caused your
petitioner though ancient to take very great pains in inquiring for
the said Burney & now finds that the said Burney was secretly
privately & in the night time carried away out of Baltimore
County as your petitioner is clearly about to make appear by one
Thomas Reynalds of this county. Your petitioner being advised that your
Worships or the Justices of each county court are to decide differences
betwixt master & servant in their respective countys and humbly
conceiving that the act aforesaid committed by the said Reynalds
is by the common law indictable and highly punishable for as
much as your petitioner is advised that a matter indictable is
only tryable in the county where the fact was comitted your
petitioner humbly requests that your Worships will cause the
said Reynalds & the boy aforesaid to be sent for and that you will
make such order in the premises as is most agreeable to law &
justice and your petitioner as in duty bound shall ever pray
                                                    Edward Smith
Which petition being duly considered by the justices aforeseaid
here in Court the day & year aforesaid it is ordered that a
summons be made out for Thomas Reynalds to be and appear
at this Court & to bring with him Thomas Burney at the same time
and the said Thomas Reynalds appearing to the said summons
it is further ordered by the Justices aforesaid that the said Thomas
Reynalds deliver unto Edward Smith the petitioner, the aforesaid
Thomas Bunney an orphan & that Edward Smith give
security to this Court that the said Thomas Burney be & appear
at the next November court to be held for Baltimore County
whereupon the said orphan is delivered and the said Edward Smith
enters into recognizances to the Lord Proprietary in the sum of
twenty pounds sterling for the said Thomas Burneys appearance
at Baltimore as aforesaid.

f.88 (DSC02213) Petition of John Paine, now blind, to be made tax free.

To the worshipfull the justices of Cecil County judicially sitting
The humble petition of John Paine of said county most humbly
sheweth that whereas your petitioner being very antient & past his
labour and it pleas'd God of late to take his eye sight from him so
that he cannot see to walk & most humbly prayes your Worships
would be pleased to remit his levey or to allow him as much tobacco
as would pay it & your petitioner as in duty bound shall ever pray.

John Paine

The which petition being duely considered by the Justices aforesaid
here in Court the day & year aforesaid it is ordered that the said John
Paine be allowed as a poor pensioner the sum of two hundred pounds
of tobacco in this present levey.

f.92 (DSC02215) Petition of Aaron Latham to have lots around court-house surveyed.

The humble petition of Aaron Latham most humbly sheweth
That whereas your petitioer being possest of the
land adjacent to the Court house land for this County
and for as much as the said marks of the said Court house
land are become blind & unknown to your petitioner as
to many others so that your petitioner cannot improve his
lands adjacent for fear of trespassing upon said
Court house land your petitioner therefore humbly prays
your worships to order the said Court lands to newly
staked & marked out with such distinct marks as may be
known to your petitioner & others for the reason aforesaid.
And your petitioner further humbly prays your worships
that if your worships think it proper your petitioner humbly
offers to clear such part of the said Court house land (as
Is no ways possest nor cultivated by any person) for that liberty
to manure the same for such reasonable time as your
Worships shall think fitt for all which your petitioner shall pray

Aaron Latham

Which petition being duly considered by the Justices
aforesaid herein Court the day & year aforesaid the said
Justices ordered that a warrant be directed from this Court

to the surveyor of this county to lay out the Court house land,
the said Aaron promises to be at the charge of putting up
locust posts and half the charge of survey.

f.94 (DSC02216 Petition of Evert Evertson for guardianship of orphan George Lewes.

To the worshipful Justices of Cecil County Court
judicially sitting - the humble petition of Evert Evertson
humbly sheweth that Mary Lewes Widow and executive of
Edward Lewes late of the said county deceased did give and
dispose of a child of the said Lewes about half a years old
a boy, unto your petitioner to serve and dwell with your
petitioner in the nature of a servant untill he should arrive
at the age of one and twenty years as it seemed to your
petitioner she had power so to do by her said husbands deceased
will, but since your petitioner has been advised to apply
themselves to your Worships in order to have the said child bound
as an orphan (as he truly is) your petitioner has under the
above notion of the Womans having full power as above
kept the child (the said boy) ever since he was a years old
unto this day and he is now five years and .. months old.
Your petitioner prays your Worships will bind the said child
unto you petitioner in the nature of an orphan. Your
petitioner humbly prays your worships out of your goodness
 will give your petitioner the offer of the said Child
he being the only one that took care of him hitherto,
And your petitioner as is duty bound will pray.

Which petition being duly considered by the Justices aforesaid
here in Court the day and year aforesaid it is ordered by the
said Justices that George Lewes aged five years old be
bound unto Evert Evertson untill the said boy arrives to
full age, the said Evert Evertson obligeth himself to learn
the said boy the trade of a rope maker and to have him taught
to read, write, and cypher as far as the rule of three, to bring him up
in the Religion of the Church of England to find him with meat,
drink, washing, lodging and apparel during his apprenticeship
and when free to give him a new suit of cloth or Drugget cloths,

a new hatt, a pair of new shoes and stockings, and two new Dowlas or
good country cloth shirts.

f.96 (DSC02217) Petition of Jonathan Bavington for release from indenture.

The humble petition of Jonathon Bavingron aged eighteen years
and upward most humbly sheweth that whereas your
petitioners father John Bavington late of the said county
deceased by his last will and testament left desired and
requested that your petitioner should be free to act and
do for himself as the age of eighteen years as by the said
will by your petitioner here ready to be produced to your
Worships may appear, but so it is may it please your Worships.
notwithstanding the said will your petitioners mother bound
your petitioner for a much longer time then by the said
will allowed unto a certain John Stoopes cordwinder who
removed out of this Province and carried your petitioner and put
him to other services than the indenture allowed him. Your
petitioner therefore humbly prays that he might be discharged
from any longer and further servitude unto the said Stoopes
or his assigns by virtue of the said indenture from his mother,
your petitioner making his allegation appearing to be true
to your worships, and your petitioner shall as bound in duty
pray.   *Jonathon Bavington*

Which petition being duly considered by the Justices
here in Court the day and year aforesaid it is ordered by the
said Justices that the petitioner be free and at his how disposal
consonant to his fathers will.

f.98 (DSC02218) Court convened 8 November 1726.

At a Court of the Right Honourable Charles Absolute
Lord Proprietary of the Province of Maryland and Avalon,
Lord Barron of Baltimore & held at Elk River for Cecil
County the eighth day of November in the twelfth year f
his said Lordships Dominion Anno Domimi seventeen
hundred and twenty six and there continued until the
fifteenth day of the same month by the Justices of sd Lordship

133

and other officers thereunto authorized & appointed of whome were

The Worshipfull

Commn'rs	Major Francis Mauldin	Mr. Stephen Hollingsworth
Present	Capt. Edward Jackson	Mr. John Baldwin
	Capt. James Alexander	Col. Benjamin Pearce

John Smith, Sheriff   Stephen Knight, Clerk

f.98 (DSC02218) Petition of John Peterson to take over Elk River ferry from Herman Kinkey.

To the worshipfull Justices of Cecil County in Court judicially
sitting – The humble petition of John Peterson most humbly sheweth
that whereas your petitioner hath for several years attended
the ferry of Elk River and hath been very faithfull, carefull
and diligent and obliging in discharging his office therein, and
also by consent of the Herman Kinkey who hither hath had
the benefit of the said ferry and is willing to yield and surrender
unto the same, It is hoped that your Worships for the aforesaid
considerations will grant give and allow the whole benefit care
charge, trust and yearly allowance of and for the said ferry
to your petitioner, he behaving himself discretely as heretofore
and your petitioner shall always as bound in duty pray.
John Peterson, Herman Kinkey.

Which petition being duly considered by the justices
aforesaid here in Court the day and year
aforesaid the same is granted, he giving security to the Courts
liking. The petitioner binds himself in recognizance twenty
 pound sterling, Thomas Biddle, Frances Foster in ten
pound sterling each (his securities) for keeping Elk ferry,
he to be allowed the usual allowance.

f.100 (DSC02219) Petition of James Christie, debtor, to be released from prison.

To the worshipfull the Justices of Cecil County in Court judicially sitting –
The most humble petition of James Christie prisoner in the custody
of the Sherriff of the said County for debt most humbly sheweth
that whereas your petitioner hath hitherto been detained for want
of an affidavit or oath made to the delivery of your petitioner his
certificates to his creditors in Baltimore county at whose suit

134

your petitioner standeth imprisoned. It is humbly hoped that your
Worships will take it into your wise considerations and grant your
poor distressed petitioner that he may(be discharged) considering the
great afflictions,maladies and indispositions of body your distressed
petitioner at present endureth, and also have now complyed with
the tenour and directions of a late Act of Assembly of this Province
made for the relief and release of poor distressed prisoners for
debt, your petitioner producing an affidavit to the delivery of
his certificates to his said creditors in due time as the said
Act directs. And your poor distressed petitioner shall always
as bound in duty pray.   *James Christie*

Which petition being duly considered by the justices aforesaid
here in court the day and year aforesaid having produced affidavit
of Doctor George Walker taken before Mr. Lance Todd, one of the
Justices of Baltimore County Court which follows in these words,
to witt: November the 4th 1726 then came George Walker
before me the subscriber one of his Lordships Justices for Baltimore Coun-
ty
and made oath that he the said Walker did deliver unto Col. Thomas
Sheridine and Christopher Bandall and severall others of
James Chrisities creditors signifying that the effects of the said
Christie were to be distributed among his creditors last August court
in Cecil county full forty days or more before the third August Court
in Cecil County. Sworne to before me. Lance Todd. ~~~ It is ordered by
the Justices aforesaid that he be discharged from his imprisonment
upon his assigning to his said creditors his debts and other
effects, whereof the Sheriff of Cecil County is to take notice.

f.101 (DSC02219) Petition of the inhabitants of north side of Sassafras for rerouting of roads.

To the worshipfull justices of Cecil County now in
Court judicially sitting, the humble petition of
the inhabitants of north side of Sassafraz River in the aforesaid County
humbly sheweth that on or about forty years ago the inhabitants
of the aforesaid County was very thin seated on the upper part of
the north side of the aforesaid river and that the publick places of the
aforesaid County as naming the Court house and houses of enter-

tainment and all other publick places as stores and such, was then
kept near the mouth of the aforesaid river and on the north side
thereof. Then was there a necessity of that road called the Lower Road
but now as it may it please your Worships since that our County has
been divided and a new Court house built in the center of the County
wide from the place it was before, and that road leads to no publick
place but is very prejudiciall to many of the inhabitants
of the north side of the aforesaid river, and that there is so many
roads and especially useless that it is almost impossible
to keep one good. Therefore we humbly pray that the road that is
the road next the river of Sassafraz may fall and that the two roads
may come into one and that it may be cleared the most direct
way from the head of Sassafraz River to Mr. Perry Phrisbys
there to joyn in the main high road that now is along the south side of
Col. John Ward plantation on the north side near the plantation
of Col. John Ward Esq. And we humbly pray that your worships may
take it into your wise and serious consideration and your
petitioners will be in duly bound ever to pray .
Richard Houghton, Nathan Sapington, Otho Otheson
Thomas Beard, Oliver Caulk, Isaac Caulk, Nehemiah Martin, Nathaniel
Hynion, Robert Nelding Sen., Robert Nelding, Jun., John Chamberling,
Phillip Stoop, Mary Shore, Nicholas Dornel, Daniel Geel...
Robert Penington, James Bowers, John Azhey, Garret Vansandt,
John Wotson, Walter Hill, Joseph Bawden, Dan Nolen, Nicholas
Vanhoware?, William Savin, Sen., Thomas Savin, William Savin,
Jun., Andrew Clements, Richard Bellew, Thomas Seerson,
James Steel.

Which petition being duly considered by the justices
aforesaid here in Court the day and year aforesaid and it is ordered
that a main road be laid out pursuant to the said petition and
cleared according to the directions of Col. John Ward and Col. Benjamin
Pearce and a special warrant directed to the overseer of North
Sassafraz Hundred.

**f.102 (DSC92220) Petition of John Dye for payment to Sarah Dye for
cleaning courthouse.**
To the worshipfull the Justices of Cecil County in Court judicially sitting –

136

The humble petition of John Dye most humbly sheweth, that whereas
it was your worships favor some time since to order Sarah Dye
should have the benefit that is allowed for sweeping the
Court house and having always done the duty required
humbly pray that the same favors may be continued and your
petitioner as in duty bound shall forever pray.

Which petition being duly considered by the justices aforesaid
here in court the day and year aforesaid the petitioner is allowed
five hundred pounds of tobacco for cleaning and sweeping the
Court house this last year and now from hence forward discharged
from that service.

f.104 (DSC02221) Petition of Elinor Ware to compel support for base-born child from its father.

The humble petition of Elinor Ware sheweth that
whereas Daniel Cook was found by your Worships and jury
to be the father of a child which if it please your Worships
your petitioner humbly produces before your Worships
and your petioner humbly prays that your petitioner
may be allowed a sufficient maintainance to be paid by
Daniel Cook to your petitioner a complete maintaince
for the said child from the birth of the same to this present
time, then your petioner shall as duty bound to pray
                         Elinor Ware

Which petition be duly considered by Justices
aforesaid here in Court the day and year aforesaid
it is ordered by the said Justices that Daniel Cook
pay unto the said petitioner nine hundred pounds
of tobacco for keeping the base born child begot
on her body by the said Daniel Cook and not to
be allowed her any more.

f.109 (DSS02223) Petition of Joseph Clerk to have stepson removed from indenture.

To the worshipful Justices of Cecil County –
The humble petition of Joseph Clerk humbly showeth

that the wife of your petitioner being in sick and very weak
condition in this year of our Lord 1722 at Susquehannah in
Cecil County did at the instigation of Enoch Enochs of this
said county put her son Kelly Warren (then aged about five
years) on apprentice and servant to the said Enoch Enochs
till he should arrive at the full age of twenty one years.
Your petitioner then being a servant to Mr. John Cappen
of the said county and not advised or acquainted of the
same humbly conceives the said child illegally bound
for which reason your petitioner prays your worships to
take it into serious consideration and dispose the said
apprentice as shall seem good to your Worships, and your
petitioner as in duly bound shall ever pray.

                                    Joseph Clerk

Which petition being duly considered by the Justices aforesaid
Here in court the day and year aforesaid it is ordered that Joseph
Clerk and his wife take into their possession Kelly Warren from
Enoch Enochs and bring him forward in June Court.

f.111 (DSC02224) Petition of Thomas Taylor for license to keep a public house.

To the Worshipfull the Justices of the Peace for the aforesaid
County at the Court held at Elk River the 13th day of June 1727 –
The humble petition of Thomas Taylor of Principio
planter humbly showeth that whereas the petitioner
being for several years past an inhabitant at the Iron
Works at Prncipio where by frequent resort of travelers
& others coming to the Iron Works & also labourers
belonging to the Iron Works and others passing and
repassing on the King's highway, the petitioner is
continually pressed upon for victuals drink & lodgings
which is much burdensome & chargeable to him by
this constant coming & going and importunities of such
as are in need of supply as aforesaid. The premises
being considered your petitioner humbly craves & begs
of your Worships (as you shall see fit in your wisdom) to
grant him License to keep a tavern or ordinary in order

to entertain or accommodate such persons as shall
require it of him, which will be a great releife to your
petitioner & may be serviceable to such as shall stand
in need of help. And your petitioner as in duty bound shall
ever pray &c ~~~

Which petition being duly considered by the Justices
aforesaid here in Court the day and year aforesaid the same
is granted he complying with the Act of Assembly, who
enters into recognizance of twenty pounds sterling for
keeping public house & Cornelius Cormack & Solomon
Rees enters themselves in recognizance of ten pounds
sterling each securitys ~~

f.114 (DSC02229) Petition of Ralph Rutter for charitable assistance with medical care.
To the Worshipfull Justices of Cecil County judicially sitting –
The humble petition of Ralph Rutter, Jun., sheweth
that your poor petitioner being reduced to the utmost
extremity humbly makes application for assistance
in his desperate condition that your Worships would be
pleased (to) take into consideration that some allowance
may be made towards the relief of your distressed petitioner
for your petitioner having spent his whole substance in
seeking after remedies and finding no relief, your Worships
I hope will please to observe that this severe affliction
is by the dispensation of the wise providence of God &
therefore hope it may be an inducement
with your goodness to consider my unhappy circumstances
and your petitioner as in duty will pray, &c
                    Ralph Rutter

Which petition being duly considered by the Justices
aforesaid here in Court the day & year aforesaid the said
Justices do allow the said petitioner three thousand pounds
of tobacco upon condition & towards payment of a Doctor
for his cure provided the same be done & if not performed
no allowance to be made &c ~~~

f.117 (DSC02230) Petition of Jeremiah Larkins for charitable assistance.
May it please your honorable Worships, I am a poor afflicted
man that has been in affliction this year & half &
am left destitute of any friends, or any help at all relying
only on the mercy of God so that I cannot subsist any longer.
I am now going under the Doctor's hands but the Doctor
is not willing to do anything to me unless that I get a note
from under your worships hands for an allowance in case
of death, so I humbly beg of your Worships to be so gracious
to take it in consideration & bestow some small allowance
upon me (your poor petitioner will forever pray &c

Which petition being duly considered by the Justices
aforesaid here in Court the day and year aforesaid the said Justices
will allow one thousand pounds of tobacco to Doctor
Rees for understanding & endeavoring a cure upon said Larkin
& if a perfect cure is made that the Court will allow
him a further consideration &c ~~~

f.123 (DSC02233) Petition of Thomas John on behalf of an abused orphan.
To the worshipfull Bench sitting for the County of Cecil
the second Tuesday in March 1728 humbly showing
that whereas there is a certain Jonathan Clark who departed
this life in the house of Thomas Preist of said County
leaving behind an orphan boy which the said Preist keeps
as by an order of the Court but grant that it be so considering the
barbarous usage the boy receives it is beyond the dictates of Christianity
to allow of, which your petitioner upon due examination
will make appear, also the said deceased Clark died intested (intestate)
and left several sorts of goods & chattels which also is in the hands
of said Preist. He reports that he lawfully administered upon the
premises which may be so, but I am sure he hath not made a
lawfull return of the inventory which upon examination I
will make appear. Also now I would have the Worshipfull bench
to take it to consideration that this poor forlorn child hath no friends
nor relations to see him righted & according to the conduct

140

of his guardians. He is likely to suffer both in body & estate
except the Worshipfull bench will take it to consideration
& appear on his behalf . As for my part I am ready to be
subservient in the matter both for God's glory & the discharge
of a good conscience as well as for that our Province & Constitution
may not come under a disgraceful collumny. And
in hopes of your Worships concurrence & your petitioner
as in duty bound shall ever pray &c ~~~

Thomas John

Which said petition being duly considered by the Justices
aforesaid here in Court the day & year aforesaid it is ordered by
the said Justices that a warrant be directed to the Constable
of Susquehannah hundred to bring the body of Thomas
Preist & the orphan mentioned in said petition during the Court
sitting &c ~~~ (No further entries regarding disposition of the case.)

f.124 (DSC02234) Petition of William Humphries for release from inden-ture.

To the worshipfull the Justices of Cecil County judicially
sitting the humble petition of William Humphries most
humbly sheweth that whereas your petitioner was
committed to the Sheriff of this County that then was, viz. Mr.
John Smith late sheriff by the order of the Honourable
the Judges of our County at a Court held for the said County
as being a criminal servant to John Higgonson of Kent
Island by which order your petitioner humbly conceives
that the said Sheriff was obliged to delivery your petitioner
to the said Higgonson which he aledgeth he did & bought
your petitioner from the said Higgonson upon which
your petitioner don't conceive himself a servant any
ways to the said Higgonson or any other person for which your
petitioner humbly prays your Worships require the said
John Smith or John Higgonson to make their claims
appear against your petitioner & your Worships judgment
therein shall oblige your petitioner to pray &c ~~~

William Humphreys

Which petition being duly considered by the Justices aforesaid
here in Court the day & year aforesaid the said Justices
are of opinion that he has served John Smith
viz. from the seventeenth day of May 1726 & should
be deemed & taken as satisfaction to this County towards
his four fold & fees, he the said Humphreys having been
convicted of felony the said John Smith promising to
satisfy the County so much towards the fees and four fold as
they shall judge his service to be worth for the time he
has served the said John Smith, but the Court not having
the judgment at present nor bring satisfied what the fees
did amount to defer further proceeding till June Court
next at which time if the said Humphreys produced the
Judgment & an account of the fees the Court will further
proceed &c ~~~

f.128 (DSC02236) Petition of Joshua George, attorney, complaining of slander by one of justices.

To the Worshipfull the Justices of Cecil
County Court – The humble petition of Joshua George one
of the attorneys of the same Court humbly showeth
that your petitioner sometime since at the request of
Mr. Edward Jennings sued Col. John Ward of Cecil County
& one of the Justices of this Court together with John Coppin,
William Sinclair, Thomas Jones, George Veazey, Henry
Ward, Josiah Sutton & Peter Bayard, Gent. That your
petitioner as attorney for the said Edward Jennings fairly
obtained a verdict & judgment in favor of the petitioner
& in pursuance of his duty issued caps ad satisfaciendum
for the damages & cost recovered. Your petitioner further
sheweth that the said Col. John Ward having heard that
executions were out has wrote to severall persons especially
some of the Gent. of this Bench reflecting on your petitioner
& withall hopeing that that your petitioner may meet with in
favour which will admit of no other constructions than
that your petitioners clients should be made sufferers in
their suits merely for that they imploy (as the said Ward
terms your petitioner) that villain, rascal or base fellow

142

Joshua George. May it please your worships your petitioner
humbly hopes that neither his clients nor this Bench have
any just occasion to complain of any undue practices of your
petitioner & your petitioner humbly hopes that his doing
his duty will not by this Bench be thought unjust &
that notwithstanding any insinuations used by the
said Col. John Ward in prejudice of your petitioner
or his clients (your petitioner is fully convinced of the
impartiality of & justice of this Bench) that so long as
your petitioner behaves himself with due obedience to
this Court & honestly to his clients he is persuaded such
insinuations will not work to his prejudice or his clients.
The affection your petitioner has to his clients just causes
moves your petitioner to address himself to your Worships
on this occasion & hopes it will be resolved this Court
that an Attorney of this Court should not receive such
usage & especially from a Magistrate for acting pursuant
to his duty & your petitioner in duty bound shall pray.
11 June 1728 ~~~~~~   Joshua George

Which petition being duly considered by the Justices
aforesaid here in Court the day and year aforesaid the said Court
is of opinion that the petitioner has done nothing but
his duty in the affair mentioned in the said petition.

f.129 (DSC02236) Petition of Neal Cooke to be made guardian of or-phan.

To the worshipfull Justices of Cecil County in Court judicially
sitting, the humble petition of Neal Cooke sheweth
that your petitioner while he lived in Pensilvania had a
young male child about three months old named William
Rudledge the son of William Rudledge committed to his
care by his parents, since which time being 12 or 13 years
past he has taken due care of the said child as one of his
own family & your petitioner about 8 years past removing
himself & family to the County of Cecil brought
with him the said child which still remains with him as one
of his family, never having any satisfaction from his parents

or others for bringing up & maintaining him & now not
having lately, to witt within some years past, heard from
the parents of said child nor knowing where they are he conceives
the said child under the care of this Court as an orphan &
pray he may be dealt with as such & bound to the petitioner
till of age, he being willing to do by him as by one of his
own family &c ~~~   *Neal Cooke*

Which petition being duly considered by the Justices aforesaid
here in Court the day & year aforesaid the said William
Rudledge the orphan therein mentioned by the said Justices
is bound unto him the said Neal Cooke until he
arrives at age, to be learned to be a farmer & the said
Neal Cooke bindeth & obligeth himself to find said
William Rudledge with meat drink washing & lodging
& apparel during his apprenticeship & to learn him to
read write & cypher as far as rule of three & to have
him instructed in the protestant religion & at his
freedom to give him two suits of cloaths the one of
broad cloth or Drugget & the other a working suit
with hats shoes & stockings equivalent & two new
Dowlas shirts also a breeding mare &c ~~~

f.134 (DSC02239) Petition of vestry of North Elk Parish for funds to repair church.

To the worshipfull the Justices of the Peace of Cecil County judicially sitting
The humble petition of the Vestry of North Elk Church sheweth
that your petitioners Parish Church & church road being very much
out of repair whereby in great measure it is rendered unfit for
the performance of the service appointed thereunto humbly pray
that an assessment of five pounds of tobacco per poll be laid on
the parishoners thereof to put your petitioners in a capacity to repair
the same with which your petitioners are not able to do the same &
your petitioners as in duty bound shall ever pray &c ~~~ By order of our
Vestry by Richard Dobson, Register.

Which petition being duly considered by the Justices
aforesaid here in Court the day & year aforesaid &
by the said Justices the parish is assessed five pounds
of tobacco per pole for the uses in said petition mentioned &c

f.136 (DSC02240) Petition of Martin Alexander for legal assistance in suit.

To the worshipfull Justices for Cecil County now in Court sitting –
The petition of Martin Alexander sheweth that whereas a
judgment was obtained against your petitioner for a considerable
quantity of tobacco more than was owing to the said Van Bebber
whereby your petitioner is greatly damnified & whereas there
is no remedy at common law your petitioner therefore humbly
prays that his case may be heard in Equity & whereas all
the attorneys in Court is retained by the said James Van Bebber
& your petitioner being ignorant & uncapable of managing
his own case your petitioner humbly prays your Worships to
assign one of the attorneys to manage the said case for me
according to the rules of Chancery & your petitioner as in
duty bound shall pray &c ~~~   Martin Alexander

Which petition being duly considered by the Justices aforesaid
here in Court the day & year aforesaid & James Calder
assigned attorney so far as lays within the jurisdiction
of this Court. &c ~~~

f.137 (DSC02240) Court convened 10 June 1729.

At a Court of Right honourable Charles Absolute
Lord & propriatory of the Province of Maryland & Avalon,
Lord Barron of Baltimore & held at Elk River for Cecil County
the tenth day of June in the fifteenth year of his said
Lordships Dominion, Anno Domini seventeen hundred &
twenty nine & there continued until the thirteenth
day of the same month by his Lordships Justices & other
officers thereunto authorized & appointed of whome were

The Worshipfull

Commn'rs	Col. John Ward	Mr. Stephen Hollingsworth
Present	Capt. Edward Jackson	Capt. James Alexander

f.137 (DSC02240) Petition of Jane Barry to have her son returned from questionable indenture.

To the worshipfull Justices of Cecil County in Court now sitting –
The petition of Jane Berry in behalf of her son Joseph Williams
humbly sheweth that a certain John Williams of the same
County unjustly holds & detains the said Joseph Williams as a servant under
pretence of sale from your petitioner for the consideration of
three pounds twelve shillings & four pence. That your petitioner conceives
herself not only to have no power of making any such disposition
but also has been always ready & intended to refund the
aforesaid sum to the said John. That the said John keeps the
said Joseph under such strict confinement that he can not
come in person to make his complaint to this Court. May it
therefore please your Worships to order such process from
this Court as may oblige the same John to appear & answer
the premises & to bring with him the aforesaid Joseph Williams
& further to do therein as you in your wisdom shall think
fitt & your petitioner shall pray &c ~~~

Which petition being duly considered by the Justices aforesaid
here in Court the day & year aforesaid it is ordered by the said
Justices that a summons be made out for John Willliams directed
to the Constable of Susquehannah hundred & also that the
said John bring with him a certain Joseph Williams this Court.

f.140 (DSC02266) Petition to reroute road in Susquehanna Hundred blocked by new settlers.

To the Worshipfull his Lordships Justices of
the peace met at the Court held at Elk River November
the 11th day 1729 – The humble petition of the subscribers
inhabiting in Susquehannah hundred humbly sheweth
that whereas a road was formerly made by consent of the neighbors
from Nottingham road by John Dawsons unto Susquehannah

146

*Lower Ferry & whereas of late we have several new neighbors
settled in our parts who have stopped up our said road
whereby we are deprived of the benefit thereof to our great
detriment loss & hindrance, that we cannot pass thereon
about our necessary affairs & business. The premises being
tenderly and wisely considered by your Worships wise & due consideration
we the subscribers do crave of your Worships that you would
grant us an order of your Court to lay out a new road from the
abovesaid John Dawsons unto Susquehannah Lower Ferry in the
most convenient way that we can find for the advantage of our
country & your petitioners as in duty bound shall ever pray &c ~~~
Samuel White, Enoch Enochs, Robert Hand, James Dillon,
Joshua Richardson, John Kersey, Samuel Brice, Cornelius McCormack,
Henry Bowen, John Sortill, Jonathan Hartshorne, John Chenoweth,
Lazarus James, Mathew Acth, John Piggot.*

*Which petition being duly considered by the Justices aforesaid
here in Court the day & year aforesaid the same is granted
& Cornelius McCormack appointed overseer of the said mentioned
In the petition &c ~~~*

f.142 (DSC02267) Petition of Inhabitants of New Munster to repair road to Elkton.

*To the worshipfull Justices for Cecil County in Court sitting
The humble petition of the inhabitants of New Munster
sheweth that there being a great necessity for
repairing the road leading from New Munster to the head
of Elk River as it was laid out by order of Court, your petitioners
pray that there may an overseer be appointed in order
to repair the said road & your petitoners shall ever pray &c ~~~*
James Alexander, James Alexander, Moses Alexander,
James Alexander.

*Which petition being duly considered by the Justices aforesaid
here in Court the day & year aforesaid the same is granted
& James Alexander, tanner, be appointed as overseer of the
roads in said petition mentioned.*

f.143 (DSC02267) Petition of Walter Cockrell for charitable support.

To the worshipfull the Justices of Cecil County now in Court sitting
The humble petition of Walter Cockrell humbly sheweth that
whereas your humble petitioner born in this County being now destitute
of the use of my limbs & daily laboring under divers other distempers
& utterly disabled from getting my living & having
not anything wherewith to support myself most humbly
prays your Worships may be pleased to take this my distressed
condition into your Worships just consideration by allowing
me with the common necessaries of life & your petitioner
As in duty shall ever pray &c ~~~

Which petition being duly considered by the Justices aforesaid
here in Court the day & year aforesaid it is ordered that henceforward
he be Levy free & that at present he be allowed two hundred
& fifty pounds of tobacco &c ~~

f.147 (DSC02269) Petition for rerouting road from Susquehanna Upper Ferry to Octoraro road.

The humble petition of Thomas Cresap ferry man of Upper
Ferry of Susquehannah River and also of severall inhabitants
near adjoining most humbly sheweth that your petitioners
labor under great inconvenience for want of having a road laid
out & established from the said ferry place into Octoraro road
near the Chapel lately built, the present (road) being moved at the
pleasure of each person who hath lands adjoining which
makes the same tedious to travellers & very troublesome to your
petitioners, wherefore your petitioners humbly pray your Worships
would appoint two neighboring persons to lay out the said road &
make a return to your Worships of the same which according to your
pleasure may be established & your petitioners shall ever pray &c ~~~
Stephen Onion, William Husband, John Chenoweth, John Piggott, William
Arindell, Nicholas Arindell, John Alling, Abraham Watson, Cornelius
Cormack, Samuel Young, William Bayley, John Mead, John Pidcock,
Joseph Young.

Which petition being duly considered by the Justices aforesaid
here in Court the day & year aforesaid the same is granted &

Mr. John Hamond & Mr. Stephen Onion appointed
Inspectors to see the said road laid out &c ~~~

f.147 (DSC02269) Petition of Nathan Phillips to recover expenses from his runaway servant.

To the worshipfull the Justices of Cecil County judicially sitting
The humble petition of Nathan Phillips sheweth that your
petitioner being run to extravagant charges by a servant of
your petitioners named George Williams who run away from your
petitioners service, your petitioner humbly prayeth redress and
your petitioner as in duty bound shall ever pray &c ~~~ Nathaniel Phillips

Aug the 21st 1725 George Williams charges at New Castle --- £ 1-2-9
July the 5th 1727 to charges at Welch Tract ---------------------- 0-10-0
Aug the 29th 1727 to charges at New castle -------------------- 1-10-6
July the 28th 1728 to charges at Chester ------------------------- 0-5-0
1725 – run away 5 days   £ 3-8-3
1727 – run away 4 days
1728 – run away 15 days
*   "   – run away 15 days*
*   29 days run away time*
Errors excepted, per me Nathan Phillips

Which petition being duly considered by the Justices
aforesaid here in Court the day & year aforesaid
the same is granted & ordered that George Williams serve
his said master or his assigns six months over & above his
time of servitude &c ~~~

f.149 (DSC02270) Petition of James Cronkelton to have his indentured servant returned.

To the worshipfull the Justices of Cecil County Court
The humble petition of James Cronklelton of Cecil County
sheweth that the twenty sixth day of June Anno
Domino seventeen hundred & twenty nine a certain Francis
Boie a youth with the consent of his parents or nearest relations
bound himself an apprentice to your petitioner for the
term of five years but so it happened that the partie that

149

wrote the bid indenture made a mistake in the year of
our Lord by not inserting the word twenty and under pretense
that the youths time is long since expired a certain
Thomas Reynolds detained your petitioners apprentice from
him tho' the youth was not born in the year one thousand
seven hundred and nine, wherefore your petitioner prays
summons may issue against the aforesaid apprentice &
Thomas Reynolds that upon hearing the allegations &
proofs of each party your Worships will determine the same
according to good conscience & your petitioner as duty
bound shall ever pray &c ~~~ James Cronkelton

Which petition being duly considered by the Justices aforesaid
here in Court the day & year aforesaid it appearing to the Court
that notwithstanding the indenture is dated in the year one
thousand seven hundred & nine yet it being proved that the
same was made in June one thousand seven hundred & twenty
nine for the term of five years & three quarters it is adjudged
by the Court that the said boy serve the said Cronkleton finding
him sufficient meat drink lodging & apparel also that he give
the said servant at the expiration of his time two suits of cloth
& a gacing(sic) loome & learne him the trade of a weaver & further
the Court adjudges that Thomas Reynolds pay the petitioner
James Cronkelton all legall costs which have accrued on the
aforesaid petition & determination &c ~~~

f.154 (DSC02273) Petition of Matthew Wallace for charitable assistance.
To the worshipfull the Justices of Cecil County Court sitting
The humble petition of Matthew Wallace of said county most humbly
sheweth that your petitioner hath been an inhabitant of the county
for a considerable number of years since during which he hath
contributed to publick payments but so it is now with your petitioner
may it please your worships your petitioner is by his misfortune
become uncapable to pay his levey, being near eighty
years of age & having no certain habitation or wherewithal to
enable him to contribute towards the defraying the County
or publick charge, your petitioner therefore humbly prays your
Worships to allow him such alms as to your Worships may seem

150

meet & your petitioner will as bound in duty pray &c ~~
Matthew Wallace

Which petition being duly considered by the Justices aforesaid
here in Court the day & year aforesaid the (petition) is granted and
allowed one hundred pounds of tobacco as an alms in the
present levey.

f.155 (DSC02273) Petition of Solomon Bowen, now blind, for charitable assistance.

To the worshipfull the Justices of Cecil County Court sitting
The humble petition of Solomon Bowen of the said
County being at the pleasure of Almighty God entirely
deprived of his sight & thereby incapable of getting his living &
being entirely destitute of all necessaries of life, both food
and raiment, most humbly prays your worships will be pleased to
take in commiseration of his melancholy condition & most
deplorable circumstances into your wise consideration &
your humble petitioner as in duty bound shall ever pray.
November Court 1730   ~~~~~   Solomon Bowen

Which petition being duly considered by the Justices aforesaid
here in Court the day & year aforesaid the same is granted
& the petitioner allowed six hundred pounds of tobacco
As a poor pention in this present levey.

f.156 (DSC02274) Petition of Thomas Chesnall for release from indenture on himself and children.

To the worshipfull the Justices of Cecil County the petition
of Thomas Chesnall in behalf of himself & his children most
humbly sheweth that your petitioner was heretofore a servant
of a certain John Stokes in which servitude
your petitioner became guilty of being lazy upon
which your petitioner was convicted & thereupon was pardoned
or reprieved by the late Governour & your petitioner further
shews that he is advised that the pardon or reprieve reinstated
your petitioner in his former state, so it is, may it please your
Worships that the said John Stokes sold your petitioner &

his children to a certain Joshua George & for a term of years not
yet expired. In tender consideration of the premises your petitioner
humbly prays that your Worships will be pleased to
enquire into the same according to Law & your conscience by
what right the said Stokes sold your petitioner & his children
& also by what right your petitioner & his children are detained
in servitude & slavery by the said George & that the said Stokes
& George true and perfect answers do make & that your Worships
give relief to your petitioner in all and singular the premises
according to Law and equity & that your petitioner & his children
be discharged from the said George & your petitioner will pray

         Thomas Chesnall

Which petition being duly considered by the Justices aforesaid
here in Court the day & year aforesaid the indenture was adjudged
good as to Thomas Chesnall for the term of thirty one years
therein mentioned & against his children untill they come
to the age of twenty one according to the indorsement
of the said indenture ~~~~

f.159 (DSC02276) Petition of John Penington for compensation for charitable expenses.

To the worshipfull the Justices of Cecil County now in
Court sitting the humble petition of John Penington of
the aforesaid County humbly sheweth that whereas a certain
Benjamin Johnson a stranger came to my house some time in
September last & was taken ill of a blood flux of which he
died & was quite destitute of every necessary either to support
him while alive or interr him when dead, I having been
at a considerable charge both in his sickness & burial &
can have no redress but by your Worships, I humbly pray
your Worships to take this my present case into your
prudent and wise consideration & your petitioner as in duty
bound shall ever pray &c   ~~~   John Penington

Which petition being duly considered by the Justices aforesaid
here in Court the day & year aforesaid the same is granted
& the petitioner allowed two hundred & fifty pounds of

tobacco in the present levey &c ~~~

f.160 (DSC02276) Petition of John McManus to be admitted as an attorney in court.

To the worshipfull Justices of the Peace now
sitting in the said county. The humble petition of John McManus
humbly sheweth unto your Worships that your petitioner
for some years practiced the Law in several of his Majesties
Courts in Ireland with some success & creditt – may it therefore
please your Worships to consider the premises & admit
your petitioner to practice in this Court & your petitioner as in
duty bound will ever pray &c   ~~~ John McManus

Which petition being duly considered by the Justices aforesaid
here in Court the day & year aforesaid the same is granted
he complying with the act of Assembly, whereupon he takes
the usual oaths & subscribes the Oath of Abjuration & Test.

f.160 (DSC02276) Petition of John MacDougall to have his fine reduced.

To Benjamin Pearce Esqr & his associates Justices of Cecil County
Court, the petition of John MacDugall most humbly sheweth
that your petitioner foolishly rashly & unadvisedly has
incurred the displeasure thereby of your Worships, the circumstances
of your poor petitioner are extreme low & poor & must
of course become a servant for the payment of that fine that
your Worships in your wise consideration thought fit to lay
upon me, tho' not adequate to the rashness & foolhardiness of
your petitioner may it please your Worships to take the
circumstances of your poor petitioner & family into your sage
consideration & be pleased to extend mercy in elevating & remitting
some part of the said fine & your petitioner as in duty bound
shall pray &c ~~~   John McDugall

Which petition being duly considered by the Justices aforesaid
here in Court the day & year aforesaid the same is granted &
half his fine is remitted as petitioned for &c ~~~

153

f.161 (DSC02277) Petition of Catherine Bryan for charitable assistance.

To the worshipfull Justices of Cecil County ~~~
The petition of Catherine Bryan most humbly sheweth
that your petitioner has for a considerable time last past
labored under a violent malady that will in the end prove
fatal to your petitioner unless your Worships take her
case into your sage consideration. Therefore your petitioner
humbly prays you would be pleased to extend your wonted clemency
mercy & charity on account of my deplorable circumstances
& your petitioner as in duty bound will ever pray &c ~~~

Which petition being duly considered by the Justices aforesaid
here in Court the day & year aforesaid the same is
granted & the petitioner allowed the sum of one
thousand pounds of tobacco as a poor pensioer in this present
levey &c ~~~

f.164 (DSC02278) Petition of Elizabeth Baker for release from false claims of indenture.

To the worshipfull Justices of Cecil County in Court sitting
the petition of Elizabeth Baker of the same County sheweth
that John Copson of the same County, Gent, claims & detains
your petitioner as a servant tho' your petitioner apprehends
herself under no tye of servitude to the same John or any other.
May it therefore please your Worships to cite the said John to
answer the premises & do therein what to you shall seem agreeable
to Justice & good conscience & your petitioner shall
pray &c ~~~   James Caldon, per petitioner

Which petition being duly considered by the Justices aforesaid
here in Court the day & year aforesaid the same is adjudged
that she is free from indenture to Mr. Copson upon
the oath of & allegation of John Darlington present
in Court &c ~~~

f.165 (DSC002279) Petition for road from Susquehanna Upper Ferry leading to Philadelphia.

To the worshipfull the Justices of Cecil County Court

The humble petition of the subscribers being some of
the nearest inhabitants to the ferry on Susquehannah
River commonly called the Upper Ferry sheweth that whereas
there is a public ferry kept backwards & forwards over
said river & being much frequented, being the nearest way
now used for the Lower inhabitants of the Province which
hath occasion to travel to Philladelphia and no direct
road leading that way but small paths very difficult
to strangers, your petitioners seeing the great need there is
of a road as well for their own use as the use of travelers
humbly prays your Worships to cause a road to be cut the
nearest & best way from said ferry place towards Philladelphia
so far as the jurisdiction of this Court as present doth extend
& to appoint a superviser to (see) said road maintained & fit for the
use intended & your petitioners as in duty bound shall pray
Robert Layor, David Layor, John McTyre, John Mitchell, John
Williams, John Hamond, Robert Porter, John Bond, John Hunter,
John McConell, Alexander McConell, David Creswell, Hugh
Barry, John Macdanel, James Paulson, Henry Touchstone, Christopher
Touchstone, James Bond, Benjamin Clease, Thomas Renshaw,
Samuel Bishop.

Which petition being duly considered by the Justices aforesaid
here in Court the day & year aforesaid the same is granted,
the petitioners clearing the road mentioned in said petition
at their own charge.

f.166 (DSC002279) Petition for laying of road north of Susquehanna Upper Ferry.
To the worshipfull the Justices of Cecil County Court the humble
petition of some of the uppermost inhabitants of Cecil County
on Susquehannah river sheweth that whereas there is a ferry
kept over Susquehannah river commonly called the Upper Ferry
& a merchants mill nearby at a place called Rocks Runn
which places being nearest navigable water that any
vessel of any considerable burthen can come up to, to
which places your petitioners is obliged to roll their tobacco,
in order to be shipt & no road laid out by order of Court which

from the upper inhabitants to said mill landing & ferry place.
Therefore your petitioners humbly pray your Worships to
order a road to be cleared & maintained from the place called
the Duck Bottom up Susquehannah river the best & nearest way
down to said Rock Runn mill & from thence to the said ferry
place & to appoint a superviser to cause said road to be kept in
good order fit for the use intended & your petitioners as in
duty bound shall pray. John Hamond, Paul Paulson, John
Williams, John Bass &c ~~~

Which petition being duly considered by the Justices aforesaid
here in Court the day & year aforesaid the same is granted &
Randall Death appointed overseer of the road mentioned in petition

f.169 (DSC02281) Court convened 9 November 1731.
At a Court of the Right Honourable Charles absolute
Lord propriatory of the Province of Maryland & Avalon
Lord Barron of Baltimore & held at Elk River for Cecil
County the nineth day of November in the seventeenth
year of his said Lordships Dominion, Anno Domini
Seventeen hundred and thirty one and there continued until
the sixteenth day of the same month & from thence
adjourned until the last day of Feb'ry & continued until the third
day of March by his Lordships Justices & other Officers
thereunto authorized & appointed of whome were

	The Worshipfull	
	Col. Benjamin Pearce	Capt. Thomas Colvill
Commn'rs	Capt. Edward Jackson	Mr. John Hamond
Present	Mr. Henry Ward	Capt. James Alexander
	Mr. William Rumsey	Mr. John Copson

John Campbell, Sheriff   Stephen Knight, Clerk

f.169 (DSC02281) Petition of Brigett Watson for charitable assistance.
To the worshipfull Justices of Cecil County Court now present
the petition of Bridget Watson who has been an inhabitant
of said County for twenty three years past most humbly sheweth
and begs leave to inform your Worships that she is now
sixty one years of age & being wholly destitute of either

husband relations friends estate money or ability of body to
labour & purchase & provide the common necessarys or
subsistence for life &c which occasions this address to your
Worships hoping you care for pity & commiserate her
poor indigent & deplorable condition as to look upon her
with bowels of compassion as an object of charity, she
having (no) other for succor or refuge & but the County which
depends upon your Worships liberality justice & merritt,
which (she) hope will be such as may extend to her relief for as
none can be more needy, & hope your Worships will remember
& believe that what you give to the poor is lent to the
Lord, so hoping your Worships will order some allowance
as is usual for your petitioner & your petitioner as in duty
bound shall pray &c ~~~~

Which petition being duly considered by the Justices aforesaid
here in Court the day & year aforesaid the petitioner is allowed
as a poor pension the sum of five hundred pounds of tobacco
in this present levey.

f.170 (DSC02281) Petition of John Hackett for charitable assistance.
To the worshipfull the Justices of Cecil County judicially
sitting the petition of John Hackett most humbly sheweth
that your petitioner being reduced by severe sickness to the
last extremity & in a manner deprived of the use of his limbs
& thereby rendered incapable of providing for his subsistence
humbly prayeth your Worships will please to assign an
allowance whereby your petitioner may be kept from
perishing, your petitioner representing himself as an object
of charity & your petitioner as in duty bound shall pray
                              ~~~~ John Hackett
Which petition being duly considered by the Justices aforesaid
here in Court the day & year aforesaid the petitioner is allowed
as a poor pension the sum of five hundred pounds of tobacco
in this present levey. ~~~~~

f.172 (DSC02282) Petition of the vestry of St. Mary Ann's Parish for funds for church repairs.

*To the worshipfull the Justices of Cecil County Court judicially
sitting the humble petition of the Vestry of St. Mary Ann's
Parish sheweth that whereas your petitioner have had some
repairs made in their church & church yard & has not anything
in hand to defray the charge therefore your petitioners
humbly pray your Worships would be pleased to grant an
assessment on the taxable persons of their parish four pounds
of tobacco p/ pole to enable your petitioners to defray the
present charge & likewise to make some other needful
repairs which is necessarily wanting & your petitioners
as in duty bound will ever pray & by order of our Vestry*

                     ~~~~~~~ p/ Richard Dobson, Register

*Which petition being duly considered by the Justices aforesaid
here in Court the day & year aforesaid the said Justices
order an assessment of two pounds tobacco per pole be levied
on the taxable of the parish mentioned in said petition ~~~~~*

f.173 (DSC22083) Petition for rerouting of roads from head of Sassafras to James Town.

*To the worshipfull Justices of Cecil County the petition of Thomas Davis
of said county humbly sheweth that the main road leading from
the head of Sasafras river to the old Court house at James Town on said
road has for many years past been very injurious to your petitioner
going through his plantation & that since the moving of the Court to
Elk river & the ferry to Peningtons Point the said road is not now so much
used as formerly and that the same road might be continued to a road
leading from the Church past your petitioners plantation & there turned
into the road leading from the Church to the aforesaid place called
James Town without prejudice to the inhabitants & would not be
injurious to travelers being so little farther than it now is that the
distance might be ridden with less trouble & fatigue than the gates
erected at the present can be opened & shut and would then be more
commodious to your petitioners plantation. Your petitioner therefore
with sundry of his neighbors, inhabitants of this County prayeth
leave to continue the said road which the church road as aforesaid
& then turn it as aforesaid into the other road at your petitioners own*

158

charge & shall ever pray &c ~~~ *William Ward, Robert Money, John*
Roberts, James McManus, John Penington, Benjamin Bonitt,
William Penington, Nathaniel Hynson, Phillip Stoops, Benjamin Davis,
Robert Penington, James Wroth, John Price, John Bateman, John Tree,
William Foster, William Freeman, Jacob Freeman, Benjamin Hastehurse,
John Johnes, Richard Healy, John Jackson, Thomas Ryland,
John Kimber, Henry White, John Cox, John Morris, Henry Hendrickson,
Thomas Wats, William Wats, James Husband, --Matts, Nathaniel Freeman
Benjamin Cox, John Dye, Christopher Denning, Thomas Ward, John Clark,
Garret Otheson, William Whettham, George Hollen, John Collins,
John Dykes, John Ward, Robert Mercer, Thomas Mercer, Sen, John Mercer,
James Lattomus, Andrew Presler, Peter Wallace, Peter Numbers,
Kinesen(?) Wroth, George Childs, John Welsh, Robert Porter, John Capen,
Athey Capen, George Greenwood, John Chambers, David Young,
William Freeman, Jun., Thomas Freeman, David Rees,
John Gullet, Thomas Severson, Henry Penington,, Sen., Henry
Penington, Jun., Thomas Jones, Tench Davis, William Riggs(?),
Nicholas Dorrel, Jacob Ozier, Abraham Hollings, Robert Otheson,
William Oldfield, Thomas Pearce, Thomas Beard, Richard Houghton,
Richard Grace, Alexander Clemens, George Woodhill,
James Collins, Daniel Benson, James Morgin, Jun.,
John Severson, Cornelius Clemens, Thomas Rodgers, Mathaias Persons,
James Kimber, Thomas Kimber, James Morgan, Sen.,
Jeffry Severson, Samuel Barnum, Rees Owing, John MacKleen,
David Rise, William Hugg, Peter Severson, Edward Burk,
Thomas Penington, Andrew Clements ~~~~~

Which petition being duly considered by the Justices aforesaid
here in Court the day & year aforesaid the same is granted.

f.175 (DSC02284) Petition of Reverend Hugh Jones for rerouting road by his house.

To the worshipfull the Justices of the Peace for Cecil County,
the petition of Hugh James Clk humbly sheweth that whereas
the road running by your petitioners door was formerly moved
that way before the Ministers house was built for the convenience
of the marsh(?) plantation which very much incomodes the
settlement at the Glebe rendering the habitation of the incumbent

*publick which ought to be private & retired, and turns the pasture into
common & exposes your petitioner and his family to the troublesome
company and insults of many drunken, swearing fellows, and makes
us unsafe in our beds, and gives opportunity for thievish negroes
and ordinary people, who continually pass that way, to corrupt
and hinder our servants, and to pilfer anything that is left out by
night, nay even to break open doors that are locked, as I have already
found by experience. Therefore your petitioner humbly
prays that an order may be granted for your petitioner to remain
within the tract of the old road and that the road may be run
around his fence to the front gate; which gate is most convenient
for coming to church considering all parts of St. Stephens parish
& the road so alterd will be as short & as good for travelers as
the road is at present & much more satisfactory &
beneficial to the incumbent. Therefore I hope your worships will
comply with this reasonable request for which your petitioner..etc*

*Which petition being duly considered by the Justices aforesaid
here in court the day & year aforesaid the same is granted.*

f.177 (DSC02285) Petition for rerouting roads in John Gilpin's Neck.

*To the worshipfull Justices of Cecil County. The humble petition of
Richard Molynoux & sundry of the neighboring people Inhabitants
of Midle(?) Neck sheweth that the horse path made out of said
neck by order of your worships whereof Mr. William Rumsey &
Dr Hugh Matthews were inspectors leads through your petitioner
Molynoux's plantation very much incomoding the
same & is a hilly bad way going through the head of a creek
which is sometimes almost unpassable by reason of high
tides & a myrie branch dangerous for man & horse in bad
weather & there might be a much leveler & more commodious
horse path made out of the same neck between the plantations
of John Wright & George Scott falling into the main
road to Sassafras, above the aforesaid Molynoux's now quarter
which would be much more convenient for the greatest part of the
inhabitants of said neck & neighbors thereabout than the
now horse path is & much to the advantage of said Molynoux's
plantation. Your petitioners therefore humbly pray your*

160

Worships order for clearing a new horse path as above described
& that the present horse path above described may be stopped
& the petitoners shall pray etc ~ Richard Molynoux, Walter Scott,
Walter Scott, Jun', Charles Scott, George Scott, Evert Everson, Evert
Everson, Jun', John Wright, Stephen Knight ~~~

Which petition being considered by the Justices aforesaid
here in Court the day and year aforesaid the same is granted the
petitioners clearing the said new road at this presents at their own
cost & charges etc ~~~

f.181 (DSC02287) Petition of Mary Rogers to have blind man made tax free.

To the worshipfull the Justices of Cecil County at the
Court house on the Elk river most judiciously sitting
The humble petition of Mary Rogers widow of Thomas
Rogers of this County lately deceased most humbly
sheweth that whereas Archibald Trumble hath
lived with my deceased husband for some years & still
remains with your petitioner & hath been blind for this
three years & not capable of doing anything by reason
of his blindness. Therefore your petitioner most humbly
prays that that she may be excused of paying the
County levey for him or at least that some provision
may be made in an allowance from the County in
lue thereof as your Wisdoms shall direct & your
petitioner as in duty bound shall pray etc ~~~

Which petition being duly considered by the Justices
aforesaid here in Court the day & year aforesaid the said
petitioner is allowed the sum of one hundred and fifty
pounds of tobacco this levey for maintaining Archibald
Trumble ~~~

f.182 (DSC02287) Petition of Joseph Moore for expenses of charitable assistance.

To the worshipfull the Justices of Cecil
County now sitting, the humble petition of Joseph Moore

of Cecil county most humbly sheweth that whereas some
time in Jan'y last past a certain Sarah Doore of the
County aforesaid came to your petitioners house and was
taken sick with the smallpox & after eight or nine
days sickness died therewith & she the said Sarah
not having any estate or effects wherewith to bury
her your petitioner was obliged to bury here at his
own cost & charge & your petitioner being a very poor
man & having a wife & four small children humbly
prays your worships will allow him something in
for the above mentioned charges & your
petitioner as in duty bound shall ever pray etc
June the 14th 1732 ~~~   Joseph Moore

Which petition being duly considered by the
Justices aforesaid here in Court the day & year aforesaid
the petitioner is allowed the sum of two hundred pounds
of tobacco this levey for the burial of Sarah Doore

f.182 (DSC02287) Petition concerning squandering of estate of John Althom.

To the worshipfull the Justices of Cecil County Court
The humble petition of Thomas & Richard Hash of the
County aforesaid humbly sheweth that your petitioners
unfortunately became bound with a certain Mary
Althom the widow of John Althom late of the county
aforesaid deceased for the due administration of the
estate of the said Althom, that since the said Mary
hath intermarried with a certain Partitias Carol Carwen
a most extravagant man that your petitioners
can clearly make appear to your worships, that
the estate is much wasted & imbesled wherefore
they pray proper redress as by the law of this Province
is directed & your petitioners as in duty bound shall
ever pray etc Joshua George p/petition ~~~

Which petition being duly considered by the Justices
aforesaid here in Court the day & year aforesaid

162

*it is ordered by the Justices aforesaid that the estate
of John Althom be delivered into their hands
immediately on their complying with the requisites
appointed by Act of Assembly they having been
sureties for the due administration thereof unless the
defendant give such security as the Court shall approve of.*

INDEX

Please note:
1 - Page numbers refer to folios (f.) in the original Court record, not pages in this book.
2 - Transcriptions have not been indexed but can be indirectly referenced through entries in the abstracts.

Cougheran, Joseph, 171
Court, John, 25
Courthouse, Sale of, 9
Courthouse, Sassafras, 4
Courthouse, Survey, 92
Cowell, John, 143
Cox, Albert, 28
Cox, Benjamin, 25, 28, 79, 89, 173
Cox, Giddion, 79
Cox, Gilbert, 107
Cox, John, 116, 173
Cox, William, 107
Creagar, James, 28
Crear, John, 143
Cresap, Thomas, 147
Creswell, David, 165
Croger, Thomas, 28
Cronkelton, James, 149
Crook, Robert, 162
Crow, William, 143
Currer, John, 11
Currer, William, 17, 25, 77
Currier, John, 171
Curtis, Jonathan , 39, 49, 52
Cuzine, George, 19
Damper/Dampeir/Dampier, Jo-anna, 58, 69, 88, 99, 119
Dare, William, 11, 12, 18, 39
Darlington, Abraham, 149
Darlington, John, 6, 164
Davis, Angell, 90
Davis, Benjamin, 24
Davis, Daniel, 64
Davis, Francis , 75
Davis, Jane, 75
Davis, Maurice, 24
Davis, Phillip, 18, 49

Davis, Tench, 173
Davis, Thomas, 173, 174
Davis, William, 24
Death, Randall, 171
Denning, Christopher, 173
Denning, Henry, 25
Dillon, James, 140, 141
Distressed prisoners, 91, 100, 121
Dobson, Richard, 17, 25, 26, 28, 48, 70, 134, 158
Dorrell/Dorrel/Dorrill, Nicholas, 28, 101, 127, 152, 173
Douglas, George, 28, 85
Dowdall, John, 0, 11, 12, 28, 65, 66, 120, 127, 132
Dowdall, Maj., 14, 78, 80
Dowding, Joseph, 161
Dowglass, George, 23
Dullon, Robert, 25
Dutch, Robert, 63
Dutton, Robert, 25
Dye, John, 102, 173
Dye, Sarah, 102
Dykes, John, 173
Earle, James, 171
Eliason, Com, 28
Emerson, Mary, 1
Enerster, Mary, 54
England, Lewis/Louis, 68, 131
Enochs, Enoch, 141
Enochson, Enoch, 6, 109, 140
Everson/Evertson, Evert, 94, 177
Execution, Hanging, 63
Eyre, Robert, 26
Farrell, Thomas, 85
Ferry, Bohemia, 2, 5, 7, 22, 37, 56, 69, 87, 157a, 162